Colonial Planning

Colonial Planning

A COMPARATIVE STUDY

BY

BARBU NICULESCU

M.A., B.SC. (ECON), PH.D.
University College of Ghana

Ruskin House

GEORGE ALLEN & UNWIN LTD
MUSEUM STREET LONDON

FIRST PUBLISHED IN 1958

This book is copyright under the Berne Convention. Apart from any fair dealing for the purpose of private study, research, criticism or review, as permitted under the Copyright Act, 1956, no portion may be reproduced by any process without written permission. Enquiry should be made to the publisher.

© George Allen and Unwin Ltd 1958

325.3
N548c

M. Govt.
March 18, 1959.

PRINTED IN GREAT BRITAIN
in 10-pt Times Roman Type
BY PURNELL AND SONS LTD
PAULTON (SOMERSET) AND LONDON

PREFACE

THIS book began as a study of development planning in the Gold Coast. The need for perspective led to a widening of the field to include other low-income territories. The need for standards of comparison further widened it to include middle-income and high-income countries. The desire for completeness led into further geographical and historical by-ways. The original study soon became submerged.

With the help of suggestions and criticisms from Sir Arnold Plant, Mr. B. Yamey and Mr. A. D. Knox the field was restricted and acquired some unity and shape, and enabled part of the material collected to be presented in 1956 as a thesis for the degree of Ph.D. in the University of London. With the additional help of suggestions from Professor F. C. Benham, Professor J. W. Williams and Dr. F. Chalmers Wright it also served as the foundation for this book. If the final structure is still deficient in form and substance it is mainly due to an innate streak of stubbornness in the author against which even the best advice is helpless.

The colonial aspect of the territories to which this work has been restricted is a rapidly disappearing phenomenon, but the impact of political changes on the underlying economic problems is slow, as the newly emergent nations well know. The major administrative contribution made by the Metropolitan Governments after the Second World War to the solution of these underlying problems has been the introduction of development planning, and this is one of the devices which the colonies have been taking over into their new-found state of emancipation and will almost certainly continue to employ. It may be hoped, therefore, that this book will still prove of some use to the student of current affairs should all the colonies reach independence to-morrow.

This study owes much to a large number of books, articles and other, published or unpublished, contributions to the discussion of the problems of development in low-income territories, and of the problem of planning. It also owes much to the kindness of many officials of various nationalities whose dispassionate views of their own problems and propensity towards unbiased and sometimes almost fierce self-criticism has been a revelation for the author. Without their co-operation and the co-operation of the institutions to which they belong this study would not have been possible. It would not be easy to specify in every instance the debt incurred to so many workers in the field. Nor would it be possible to attempt a full bibliography of all the books and articles relevant to this study. To be of real help to the reader, such a bibliography would have to be an annotated list, and that work has been done, and done well, elsewhere. The bibliography at the end of the book has therefore been restricted to the official publications and memoranda directly concerned with the development plans in the relevant territories, and to some of the published work which has been quoted within the text, or which has provided some specific argument used in this study.

Margaret Niculescu has extracted most of the quotations used, has compiled the bibliography and the index, has checked the proofs, and has made comments and criticisms which have led to many minor and some major revisions and rearrangements.

CONTENTS

PREFACE *page* 5

PART I: INTRODUCTION

1. A GENERAL SURVEY OF COLONIAL DEVELOPMENT PLANS 13

    The comparability of development plans. Capital formation and outside contributions. Criticisms of the metropolitan contributions

PART II: BACKGROUND TO PLANNING

2. OBSTACLES TO THE ECONOMIC DEVELOPMENT OF THE COLONIAL TERRITORIES 27

    Social frameworks not adjusted to modern techniques. Modern techniques not adjusted to local conditions: in agriculture, outside agriculture. The burden of income and output disparities

3. OBSTACLES TO ECONOMIC PLANNING IN THE COLONIES 36

    Overburdened administrations unaccustomed to planning. Economic artificiality of administrative units

4. POLICIES FOR DEVELOPMENT 45

    Introduction of new techniques: small-scale production. Introduction of new techniques: large-scale production—public works, mining, industries. Balanced growth and external economies

PART III: AN HISTORICAL OUTLINE

5. THE GROWTH OF THE IDEA OF DEVELOPMENT PLANNING FOR COLONIAL TERRITORIES 57

    The British experience:

    A. *Changes in metropolitan policies:* Treasury grants and Colonial loans, The Empire Marketing Board, The 1929 Colonial Development Act, The Moyne Commission and the 1940 Colonial Development and Welfare Act, Wartime

retrenchment and the 1945 Colonial Development and Welfare Act, The increasing importance attached to planning.
B. *Changes in the policies of the colonial territories:* The pre-1940 experience, The West Indies planning experiments, The beginning of generalised territorial government planning.
The French experience: The French Imperial Conference of 1934–5, Post-war plans. The Belgian experience. The Netherlands experience.
The general acceptance of planning.

PART IV: PLANNING MACHINERIES

6. THE METROPOLITAN GOVERNMENTS' PLANNING MACHINERIES — 79

    Britain. France. Belgium and the Netherlands

7. THE TERRITORIAL GOVERNMENTS' PLANNING MACHINERIES (I): A CASE STUDY — 88

    A case study—Kenya:
    Approach to development planning, Collection of basic information, Setting up the Development Committee, Implementation of the plan, Revision of the plan, New collection of data, Appointment of new planning committee and abolition of Standing Planning Committee and of DARA, New plan, New Development Committee and further reorganisation of the implementation stage.
    Conclusions

8. THE TERRITORIAL GOVERNMENTS' PLANNING MACHINERIES (II): A COLLECTION OF DATA — 95

    (*a*) Relating to expenditure: The 'departmental' approach, The 'problem' approach
    (*b*) Concerning resources

9. THE TERRITORIAL GOVERNMENTS' PLANNING MACHINERIES (III): PLANNING BODIES — 104

10. THE TERRITORIAL GOVERNMENTS' PLANNING MACHINERIES (IV): IMPLEMENTATION OF THE PLAN — 110

    Financial control: Development reports, Development budgets, Development funds. Supervisory authorities

CONTENTS 9

11. THE TERRITORIAL GOVERNMENTS' PLANNING
   MACHINERIES (V): REVISING BODIES 118
   The need for more detailed basic data

PART V: ANALYSIS OF THE PLANS

12. PLANNING PERIODS, RESOURCES AND PRIORITIES 125
   Planning periods: Ten year plans, Short plans, Variable periods, Interim plans
   Planning resources: CD & W funds, FIDES, Prosperity Fund and the Ten Year Plan Fund, Loans, Local revenues, Planning resources arising from the planned development
   Priorities: Reconstruction and development

13. THE METROPOLITAN GOVERNMENTS AND THE
   PROBLEM OF PRIORITY ALLOCATION 138
   Advice from the metropolitan government—Britain: Economic viability and the standard of living, Views on individual priorities
   Decisions by the metropolitan government—France

14. THE TERRITORIAL GOVERNMENTS AND THE
   PROBLEM OF PRIORITY ALLOCATION 149
   The administrative units, The commonsense versus the scientific approach, Pet projects versus general expansion, The problems of capital investment and of recurrent cost planning, Treatment of cross-effects as negligible, Human resources and natural resources, Priority patterns in the social services. Extension versus quality

15. SOME INDIVIDUAL PRIORITIES 163
   Communications
   Agriculture

PART VI: CONCLUSIONS

16. CONCLUSIONS 177
   The non-controversial achievements of the plans. The controversial aspects of the plans: Criticisms of content, Criticisms of form. Future possibilities

APPENDIX I: Areas and Populations 189

APPENDIX II: Select Bibliography 194

INDEX 205

PART I
INTRODUCTION

CHAPTER 1

A General Survey of Colonial Development Plans

THE seventy-odd territories touched upon in this work (their number has varied over the last few years due to mergers, subdivisions or change of status) cover a total area of some 6·2 million square miles, have an estimated total population of some 133 million, and an estimated total gross national product of some £4,700 million.

TABLE I

	National Product		Population[e]		Area[e]
	£ million	Year	Millions	Year	(million square miles)
Belgian Congo and Ruanda Urundi	410[a]	1955	17·4	1956	·936
British territories	3,000[b]	1956	83·0	1956	1·960
French territories	1,250[c]	1956	32·6	1957	3·236
Surinam (Dutch Guiana)	20[d]	1955	·2	1955	·056

(a) Cf. *Rapport de la Banque Centrale du Congo Belge et du Ruanda Urundi*, 1956, p. 40.
(b) Cf. *Cmd 195*, 1957. Calculated from data on p. 86.
(c) Cf. P. Moussa, *Les chances économiques de la communauté Franco-Africaine*, 1957, p. 139.
(d) Estimate based on data from *Ten Year Plan for Surinam*, 1954, p. 24.
(e) Cf. Appendix I for more detailed data.
For the conversion of the various currencies the following rough exchange rates have been used: £1 = 10 N.Fl. = 140 B.Frs. = 1,000 Fr.Frs.

The political status of the seventy-odd territories is, or has been until recently, what might be roughly called 'colonial'. With the exception of the marginal cases of Cyprus, Malta and Gibraltar, and of some very small units, like St. Pierre et Miquelon, they are situated in the tropical regions; and their governmental policies have included in most cases attempts at preparing and implementing longer-period development plans. In this work development plans of some sixty of these territories have been taken into account. Hong Kong, with an estimated mid-year 1956 population of some 2·4 million, is the only territory of some size for which no development plan has been drawn up. The total estimated mid-year 1956 population of the other 'non-plan' territories, all of them British, did not reach half a million.[1]

All these territories are usually described as under-developed, and many of them are held to be under-populated. The latter two terms are both relative terms and need some expounding.

'Under-development' ought to refer to the development potentialities within a reasonable, foreseeable future of the population group under discussion. It makes little sense from the point of view of practical economics to define the 'under-development' of one group in terms of either the present-day standards or of the potentialities of another group which has different natural or human resources, including different levels of skills and capitalization. Though it is to be hoped, maybe even expected, that standards of output and consumption will in time be equated throughout the world, discussions of the problem of economic development in terms of such expectations are still sufficiently eschatological to be the rightful domain of the visionary.

It is at least arguable that some of the territories mentioned here may have reached a stage of development as advanced as is feasible given their natural resources and their potentiality for the improvement, through their own unaided efforts, of their productive equipment in capital and in skills. This seems indeed to have been the view of the experts and of the statesmen who have managed to convince the colonial powers involved of the necessity of providing metropolitan funds and skills to enable these territories to overcome their state of stagnation. If under-development is taken to mean what it seems to imply—a potentiality for further development—the rather pleasing paradox may be put forward that it is outside help which has transformed many 'fully developed' into 'under-developed' territories.

The concept of under-population, almost as widely accepted as that of under-development, is not necessarily much more helpful for purposes of analysis, though it is equally useful as a vague umbrella term. Like under-development, under-population must be referred

[1] For a list of the territories, their areas and populations, see Appendix I.

both to the natural resources of a territory and to the capital and skills of the population group under discussion. But it has a further drawback: it tends, much more than 'under-development', to concentrate the attention on a *territory* instead of on the population group, which should be the economist's main concern. There is thus the tendency to call an empty piece of potentially fruitful land 'under-populated', though it might be exceedingly difficult to find an economically sound way by which population could take it over. Such land might much more reasonably be called reserve land into which expanding populations could at some future stage gradually overspill without involving uneconomic or socially unacceptable efforts.

The relative popularity of the use of the concept of under-population in connection with the territories under discussion has, nevertheless, a firm foundation in economic facts. It represents an attempt at isolating a feature common to practically all these territories, and which is of importance in understanding some of their difficulties: the smallness of internal markets. This in turn is often due to the fact that most of these territories are 'over-spaced'. A clear example of this problem is that of the West Indies. Individual islands in the West Indies are often described as 'over-populated' or even as 'grossly over-populated'. Attempts at solving their problems by the diversification of each island's economy have had little success: the local markets are much too small. The only real solution appears to be the integration of all the islands into one single market, combined with some specialization in production, island by island. One island would concentrate on sugar cane, another on dairy farming, another would become an industrial centre, and so on. The difficulty in reaching this goal is that of the lack of easy transport between these widely separated small units. There is little economic difference between the problems of these islands, separated by an expanse of ocean, and those of population groups in the centre of 'under-populated' Africa, similarly isolated, though in their case by stretches of empty land, and similarly compelled to renounce specialization.

THE COMPARABILITY OF DEVELOPMENT PLANS

The broad similarities listed above between the territories under discussion may give the impression of a greater degree of homogeneity than actually exists. There is a specially strong temptation to assume that it might be possible to devise methods of comparing development plans, and results, as between the different territories, and even of summing them up. It is exceedingly doubtful, even if such an exercise were technically possible—if, that is to say, development plans covered similar items, in similar terms, over the same periods of time, and if their results were assessed in similar ways—whether comparisons of the plans as a whole would, except in a few odd cases, make much economic sense, as items *outside* development plans tend to vary greatly and to have powerful impacts on the speed of development. But, in fact, this is just idle speculation. Development plans in the various territories have not covered the same items, or the same periods, have not used the same terminology, and little attempt has been made by administrators or experts of any description to assess their results. The most that can be done is to outline the main views held concerning the effectiveness of different policies in limited economic sectors, or of a combination of such policies. Agricultural development could thus be based on large-scale mechanization, or on extension services and other ways of encouraging small-scale private farming; or on a mixture of both; and main transport arteries may be considered as alternative or as complementary to feeder roads.

The estimates given in Table I as well as in the rest of this chapter should therefore be taken for what they are: a collection of heterogeneous data which will only bear comparison in the vaguest way and which no doubt could be used as ammunition for arguments, but for little else.

The quality of the existing information concerning the resources devoted to development plans varies greatly. In the case of the British territories tables have been published annually indicating expenditures contemplated by the colonial governments under the current development plans.[1] But these plans may cover anything from complete budgetary provisions, including both recurrent and capital expenditure for a number of years ahead, for some territories, to part only of a capital investment programme for others. Nor do such plans guarantee a close conformity between the contemplated and the actual expenditure. Especially misleading have been the breakdowns into the expected sources of finance. A large-scale increase in the local resources during the early stages of the plans due to increased prices for raw materials, combined with delays in the execution of the plans and thus with the postponement of expenditure, and with difficulties in raising internal and external loans, have made the proportion of loan finance in the case of many plans have

[1] Cf. Appendix III in *The Colonial Territories*, an annual Colonial Office Command Paper, and especially *Cmd 9489*, 1955, and *Cmd 195*, 1957.

little relation to what had been originally contemplated and published.

In the case of the French territories published data include only development projects financed (wholly or in part) with metropolitan funds. There has been no official attempt to tabulate the sums contemplated, or actually spent, by each territory on projects which have been separately financed, even if such projects were part of a general territorial development programme. This omission has been of less importance in their case than it would have been in that of the British territories because (with the exception of two or three territories, such as the Ivory Coast and the Cameroons) the proportion of local resources devoted to development under the plans has tended to be small, and in many cases insignificant, compared to that in the much richer British territories.

The Belgian Congo, Ruanda Urundi and Surinam have so far had only one development plan each, which eliminates the problem of comparability between plans over time, though even in the contiguous and economically complementary territories of the Belgian Congo and Ruanda Urundi the respective plans cover different periods.

CAPITAL FORMATION AND OUTSIDE CONTRIBUTIONS

It is to some extent simpler, having in view the available data, to attempt a summary of total capital investments and of the financial contributions made by the metropolitan countries for purposes of development.

In the British territories an attempt has been made, under the guidance of the Colonial Office, to collect and tabulate on an annual basis comparable information on capital formation. Published regularly since 1955, it covers the major forms of physical assets of most types of investors within the money economy. The capital formation occurring outside the money economy, such as village housing, tools made by local craftsmen and the extension of cultivated areas, is, on the other hand, almost entirely excluded.[1] The investment in gross fixed capital in 1956 has been estimated to be of about £470 million (or £440 million excluding Hong Kong), a 75 per cent increase at stable prices over 1948. The estimate for 1956 for *local* saving plus provision for depreciation in the colonial territories, excluding Hong Kong, is of some £350 million.[2]

[1] Cf. *Cmd 9489*, p. 59.
[2] Cf. *Cmd 195*, 1957, pp. 85–6.

This may be compared with the Colonial Development and Welfare grants to the colonial territories made by the United Kingdom over the eleven years since the start of generalized development plans (that is, between April 1, 1946, and March 31, 1957) of some £137 million; with the total borrowings by the colonial governments on the London market (not necessarily within development plans) from the end of 1946 to May 1957 of some £163 million; and with the Exchequer advances to the Colonial Development Corporation outstanding on May 31, 1957, of some £54 million; or a total under these three headings of some £354 million.[1]

This does not, of course, give a complete picture of the financial contributions from the United Kingdom to the economies of the colonial territories. Private capital flowing into the colonial territories has thus been estimated, with 'varying degrees of reliability', at a total of some £190 million over the three years 1954–6.[2] It is a fair assumption that most of this capital will have been investment capital.

It is more difficult to interpret the significance for economic development of the grants-in-aid and of the issues for specific purposes, including loans, by the United Kingdom Government through the Vote for Colonial Services. These grants-in-aid and issues amounted in 1956–7 to £19 million out of a total vote of some £26 million, and included items covering expenditures due to a state of emergency, such as those in Cyprus, Malaya, or Kenya; hurricane damage expenditure, as for Jamaica, British Honduras and Grenada; general financial aid, as for Malta; and special project loans or grants, such as for airports or surveys.[3] The share attributable to the colonial territories of the United Kingdom military expenditure is, of course, impossible to calculate exactly, though an estimate of some £100 million a year has been made by Professor Benham.[4]

Contemplated expenditure over the next few years by British colonial governments and other local public bodies for development purposes, within or outside development plans, is estimated at some £150 million a year. Of this about £15 million will come from territorial allocations by the United Kingdom Government under the CD & W schemes; some £45–50 million will, it is hoped, be raised as

[1] Cf. *House of Commons Paper No. 200*, 1957, Statement V, p. 39; *Economic Development in the Commonwealth*, HMSO, 1956, p. 68; and *Cmd 237*, 1957, paras. 18, 29.
[2] Cf. *Cmd 195*, 1957, Table 24, p. 79.
[3] Cf. *Cmd 195*, 1957, pp. 87–8.
[4] *Financing the Economic Development of Under-developed Countries*, United Nations Association, 1955, p. 33.

loans—£30 million from external sources (including the London market and the International Bank) and the rest through local loans (including currency funds, other special funds, marketing boards and semi-public issues); and the remaining £85–90 million from local revenues and the use of reserves. It is thus expected that some £105 million, or over two-thirds of public expenditure on development, will come from local sources.[1]

In the French territories capital formation in 1956 may be estimated at some £150 million. £57 million have been provided as grants by the French Government through the 'Fonds d'Investissement et de Développement Économique et Social des Territoires d'Outre-Mer' (FIDES) and £16 million as long-term loans through the 'Caisse Centrale de la France d'Outre-Mer' (CCFOM).[2] Of the rest, it is estimated that rather less than half has been provided by local public authorities and the remainder by private sources.[3]

Though the coverage of the private sources is not clear, it may include a wider section than that included in the estimates already quoted for the British territories, as some account seems to have been taken of at least the more 'productive' of the investments in the non-money economy, such as the extension of cultivated land or plantations by self-employed labour.

The total contributions by France to investments in the overseas territories between April 30, 1946, and December 31, 1956, have amounted to some £440 million of direct grants by FIDES, and to some £125 million as long-term loans by CCFOM—a total of £539 million. On the assumption that these sums represent slightly less than half the total investments over that period, the total capital formation may be estimated to have averaged a little over £100 million a year.

As in the case of the British territories, government grants, subsidies and loans must be added to the actual investment funds for purposes similarly ranging from hurricane damage grants to budget subsidies. The total for the French Union under this heading amounted to some £33 million in 1955, of which some £6·1 million were directly attributable to the overseas territories dealt with here.

---

[1] Cf. *Cmd 195*, 1957, p. 84.
[2] Data from internal CCFOM papers.
[3] Cf. P. Moussa: *Les chances économiques de la communauté Franco-Africaine*, 1957, p. 127, fn. 9, and p. 149, fn. 12. Investments by local public authorities have been estimated at £27 million in 1954 and £32 million in 1955, compared to metropolitan public investments in the same territories of £69 million and £72 million respectively (op. cit., p. 125); precise data for 1956 are not yet available.

In addition, some £43 million were spent during the same year in these territories for the armed forces.[1]

In Surinam the development plan under way provides for the expenditure of some £25 million over ten years. About one-third of this sum will be provided by the Surinam Government, one-third by the Netherlands Government and one-third raised in the form of loans with Netherlands Government guarantee. The Prosperity Fund of Surinam of some £4 million set up by the Netherlands Government in 1947 was officially wound up on March 31, 1955, and some of the projects undertaken by it have been incorporated in the 1955 ten-year plan.[2] Between 1947 and 1964 inclusive the Netherlands Government will thus have contributed up to £12 million in direct development grants or some two-thirds of a million pounds a year, and will have provided guarantees for loans of some £8 million. It is not possible as yet to provide an estimate of total annual capital formation in Surinam.

The Belgian Congo (and Ruanda Urundi) have had an estimated gross capital formation of £576 million between 1950 (the beginning of the Congo ten-year plan) and 1956 inclusive. Of this, £234 million have been public investments. Over the four years 1952–5 inclusive the estimated average gross capital formation has been fairly stable at some £110 million a year, though the proportion of public to private investment has varied within this total from 60 per cent to over 80 per cent, with a peak in 1954 of over 90 per cent. Total loans from abroad during this period have amounted to an average of slightly over £12 million a year, or to about 11 per cent of total investments. In 1950 and 1951 the Belgian Congo had, on the other hand, invested abroad a total of £38 million, or only £10 million less than its total borrowing over the following four years.

The Belgian Government has made no direct grant to either territory since the start of their respective plans (1950 for the Belgian Congo and 1952 for Ruanda Urundi), but it has so far advanced, free of interest, loans amounting to over £19 million to Ruanda Urundi. In addition it has guaranteed various loans, including International Bank loans, raised by the Congo Government on the Belgian or on foreign markets.

Investments under the two plans have been of some £210 million in the Congo between 1950 and 1956 inclusive, and of some £13

---

[1] Cf. *op. cit.*, p. 130, 131, fn. 17.
[2] Cf. Stichting Planbureau Suriname: *Verslag 1954–6 Tienyarenplan Suriname*, 1957, vol. 2, pp. 14 ff; and *Samenvattend Eindverslag van het Welvaartsfonds Suriname*, 1955, p. 5.

million in Ruanda Urundi between 1952 and 1956 inclusive, though part of the expenditures in the case of the latter cover also certain individual projects started as early as 1949.[1]

Total capital formation in the British, French and Belgian territories in 1956 may thus be very roughly estimated at some £730 million, of which at least £180 million originate from the metropolitan powers concerned. How much bigger than this the metropolitan contribution actually is depends on the size of local reinvestments by private enterprises of metropolitan origin and, of course, by the share of the extraordinary contributions from metropolitan sources for purposes of defence, etc., which might be accepted as capital formation in the economic sense. In terms of the total gross national product, capital formation therefore amounts to a little under 16 per cent and the metropolitan contribution to it to at least 4 per cent, or slightly over a quarter.

CRITICISMS OF THE METROPOLITAN CONTRIBUTIONS

Certain queries have been raised in connection with the metropolitan contributions to the economic development of the colonial territories. Specific to the relationship between the United Kingdom and the British colonial territories is what has been called by certain critics 'Point Five' (defined as the reverse process to that of President Truman's 'Point Four'); that is to say, the investment of colonial funds in the United Kingdom. The total of sterling assets held by the colonial territories at the end of 1956 amounted to £1,454 million. Sterling balances of these territories have increased between 1950 and 1956 by an estimated £672 million.[2] This is more than double the United Kingdom funds invested through official channels in the colonies during that period, and possibly the equivalent of the total official and private investments. It could thus be argued, as has in fact been done, that all that has happened is that some of the colonial territories have financed the capital formation undertaken in others via the United Kingdom financial market.

This analysis, taken at its face value, gives a rather erroneous impression of the underlying economics of the transactions between

[1] Cf. *Rapport de la Banque Centrale du Congo Belge et du Ruanda Urundi*, 1957, Table 39 on p. 80; p. 84; Table 43 on p. 84; and Table 49 on p. 89.
[2] Cf. Prof. F. W. Paish: 'Britain as an Exporter of Capital to Under-developed Countries', Table 4, in *Financing the Economic Development of Under-developed Countries*, United Nations Association, 1955; and cf. Cmd 195, 1957, p. 80, Table 25.

the United Kingdom and the colonial territories. The United Kingdom Government grants to the colonial territories are not reversible. The most that could be argued in terms of the preceding analysis is that the 'loans' from the colonial territories temporarily offset these grants which therefore did not have to be paid for by the United Kingdom in real economic terms at the time when they were entered in the books. The actual handing over of resources equivalent to the grants will in fact take place when the colonial territories decide to recall their loans to the United Kingdom. The past CD & W grants could therefore be looked upon as a generous gesture made by the Britain of yesterday but which will have to be paid for by the Britain of tomorrow.

When the financial transactions between the United Kingdom and the colonies are looked at more closely further objections to the 'Point Five' approach become apparent. The colonies will always find it convenient to hold a certain amount of capital in as liquid a form as possible while at the same time deriving some revenue from it. The London market provides the best facilities in this direction. For the reverse movements of capital, it is normal to expect that United Kingdom investors will be drawn to the colonial markets in accordance with the relative profitability of colonial investments. Only a peculiar view of economic transactions can raise problems of intergroup ethics in either of the above two cases.

An exception could be found, at first sight, in the case of the compulsory sterling holdings in the United Kingdom (on Colonial Office instructions) by the Currency Boards in the colonial territories. The weakness even of this case lies in the fact that the other surplus funds held in London by the territories whose currency board holdings are large tend to be appreciable. In other words, even if there had been no such compulsion to have a sterling equivalent of local currency issues, such an equivalent or more would probably have been held, in any case. Though this position may change in the future, it must not be forgotten that two types of internationally acceptable currency must always be kept by any community indulging in international trade. First, such a community must have sufficient means to pay for day-to-day imports and to allow of short-term movements of funds. (This may, of course, be replaced in certain cases by longer-term reciprocal clearing or payments arrangements, with settlements only at the end of an agreed period.) Secondly, such a community must have the necessary reserves to settle its debts arising from longer-term adverse movements of trade and of capital transactions. (No clearing arrangements can deal with this.) The British colonial territories must be able to deal with both types of payments when they arise from transactions within the sterling area, and their reserves must be correspondingly ample. Payments arising from transactions with the rest of the world are, of course, dealt with as part of the payments for the sterling area as a whole and are covered by the area's total resources or by the area's payments agreements.

A rather different criticism of metropolitan investment policies has been raised mainly in connection with French policy, but some of it could and has been voiced also in the case of the investment policies, some metropolitan and some local, in the other colonial territories.

Part of this criticism is purely emotional and arises from the normal touchiness of people who are in the rather awkward relationship of givers and receivers. It is obviously further complicated when additional problems of awakening national consciousness and pride are involved. Certain statements by the giver can very easily be construed as self-praise or as offensive expressions of condescension to the receiver, leading in return to not necessarily relevant analyses of the grants in terms either of the giver's wealth or of the receiver's 'real' needs.

But part of the criticism is much more precise. As stated in the case of the French investments, it raises two main points which have to be discussed on their merits.[1] First, it argues that investments have been mainly directed so as to benefit the French metropolitan enterprises and their French managers or shareholders, or the French immigrants; similar criticisms have also been put forward in the case of the Belgian territories—where the funds involved are, furthermore, local funds—and in that of quite a few of the British territories. Secondly, it argues that the total size of the investments in money terms in public works and in subsidized industrial or agricultural developments has little connection with the real value of such investments because, due to wrong economic conceptions or inefficiency or both, these investments tend to be of comparatively small benefit to the populations concerned. They may even prove economic burdens owing to their imposition on the community of upkeep and maintenance costs out of proportion to their economic returns. Both these criticisms have been accepted as valid in individual cases not only by outside impartial observers but even by responsible local or metropolitan administrators. But it is possible, and in certain cases justifiable,

[1] Cf., among many others, 'Le fonds d'investissement et de développement économique et social dans les territoires d'outre-mer', article in *Présence Africaine*, No. 11, 1956, and No. 12, 1957.

to refuse to look at the results of isolated individual projects or to judge even a wider programme of development on its immediate effects, and to ask that the development efforts should be envisaged from the point of view of their overall and of their long-term results. Such an approach, of course, makes it difficult to draw even approximate quantitative conclusions concerning the effectiveness in the short run of the metropolitan contributions (or even of the whole of a development programme) in raising the productivity and the standards of living of the native populations concerned. It will, no doubt, for this reason long continue to provide a very fruitful though not always very enlightening field for keen controversy.

PART II
BACKGROUND TO PLANNING

CHAPTER 2

Obstacles to the Economic Development of the Colonial Territories

THE colonial territories have come to rely for capital equipment, techniques, manufactured consumption goods and to a fair extent finance on the industrially more advanced countries, especially on those of the 'western type'. The impact of the western economic and social systems on those of the colonial territories is thus strong. Development planning in those territories must therefore take into account the need for the mutual adaptation of the independently developed features of the western, rich and technically advanced communities on the one hand, and of the colonial, poor and technically backward communities on the other.

Whatever the western systems to be introduced, capitalist, socialist or communist, many of the social and economic strands in existence in the colonies will have to be cut and new connections established. Social and economic changes take place continuously throughout the world, but in the communities which have already settled down to the modern systems of production and distribution, changes, however many and rapid, affect the foundations of the society only through a process of erosion. In addition, they have the advantage of being generated from within and therefore automatically adjusted to the general structure of the community. In colonial territories, on the other hand, they affect a much broader band of relationships, some of them in a fundamental manner. Their sometimes brutal impact on the local social fabrics may be primarily the concern of the sociologists or of the politicians; but the effects on economic development of the resistance, natural to any organism, to changes imposed from outside is of direct interest to the economist. A lack of awareness of the importance of such resistance to change can lead to nonsensical measures and unfortunate results.

Much has already been written by economists, sociologists and anthropologists on these problems of change and their possible solutions. The items discussed below have been chosen as the most significant or interesting to a student of administratively planned development. The list is obviously arbitrary and the reader is not expected to agree with its every detail. But these are the kind of problems which have had to be faced, even if not always explicitly, by the planners. Whether or not development plans have attempted to tackle them, an awareness by the student of their existence is therefore important for a fuller appreciation of the climate of opinion surrounding the planners, of certain of the administrative problems discussed further on, and of the plans themselves.

SOCIAL FRAMEWORKS NOT ADJUSTED TO MODERN TECHNIQUES

The traditional systems of production and distribution in most of the colonial territories seem to have been largely based on the accepted paramountcy of group security. The methods of production and distribution developed over the past centuries in the western nations have been increasingly based, at least until very recent times, on the idea of individual risks and profits. The introduction of western methods in the colonies could only be successful if either a new system of social relations, including social supports and sanctions, is established on something like the western pattern or if the western techniques are adapted to the traditional relations. It is of course possible to have halfway houses both in the sense that only certain groups in society may have to adopt the new methods and the implied changes in their social and economic relationships, or that it might be possible to evolve some new system of production and distribution which, though based on the western techniques, could fit into the local social and economic relations. (There is, of course, also the possibility of a blue-print for an entirely new type of society, but this is outside my scope.)

The following socio-economic relationships seem to make the spread of western methods of production especially difficult.

There is, first, a tendency to *communal ownership* of land and a resulting difficulty in establishing clear titles of ownership vested either in an individual or in a legal person. Much of present-day agricultural production for the market, to be efficient and profitable, has to be undertaken by individuals on land to which they must have secure title if they are to undertake the necessary improvements. The problem of land ownership becomes even more important in the case of industrial and urban development, and the lack of clear titles and of simple systems of exchange are one of the main deterrents to such development in many of the colonies. This has been especially the case in the British territories, where legal 'interference' with native laws and customs has been frowned upon.

There are, of course, cases even in agriculture where communal ownership need be no deterrent if a certain amount of rationalization is introduced in the productive activities. The 'factory' system of production from the land (either through systems of communal irrigation or in plantations) had been pioneered in tropical countries long before the Soviet attempt to introduce it in more temperate climates and the notion of individual ownership is not necessary to its success. But attempts to extend such systems based on communal ownership throughout the economy in every conceivable combination of natural and population factors and for every conceivable type of product and market would be unreasonable and lead to the same negative results as have all-or-nothing attempts elsewhere.

There are, secondly, systems of relationship between the individual and the group which differ significantly from those in the western communities. There is thus a widely accepted system of *group interdependence* by which the group tends to be more important than the individual, so that, while a laggard individual is being dragged along by the group, the more active individual will be expected to drag the whole group after himself. This does not only make capital investment by the more active individuals difficult, because so much more of their available income must be spent on consumption goods as a help to other members of the group, but it also acts as a deterrent to heavier exertions by such individuals. This obstacle may sometimes be over-emphasized, but nevertheless it has to be taken into account. One of its results is that individuals who 'make good' tend to do so away from their own group, which leads to the rather peculiar phenomenon that the main investing classes in each group tend to be strangers from the group; and, as there is more temptation for people to move away from poorer to richer communities than vice-versa, that it is members of the poorer communities who thus tend to become the well-to-do even within the richer communities.

This obstacle will only be overcome gradually, but there is little doubt that it will be overcome quite naturally. Increasing migration, even over comparatively short distances; estrangement from the group, due especially to education away from or out of it for its children; the increasing acceptance of creeds, such as Christianity or Mohammedanism, which base themselves on biological families and not on groups; and the increasing provision by the State of the facilities for which help is most often demanded from the richer members of the groups and most difficult to refuse, such as education and health—should all contribute to a lessening of the individual's responsibility for the group.

There can be, at the opposite extreme, a complete lack, at least for the men, not only of group but even of family responsibility. This still seems to affect a large proportion of the population of the West Indies and is a left-over from the days of slavery, when slaves were not allowed to set up families. Such an atomized society is not conducive to that desire for personal accumulation and investment which is a necessary feature of non-communist societies if a rapid increase in output is to be attained.

Certain *systems of inheritance* also fit with difficulty into an economic framework based on individual ownership and individual savings. This applies especially to the matrilineal systems of inheritance which deprive a man's children in favour of his brother, or of his sisters' children; and it is also of some importance in polygamous societies where wealth is correlated with a large number of wives and children and hence tends to be consumed, thus preventing the formation of investment nuclei.

The possibility of a *lack of incentives* may also be profitably discussed here. Though it affects primarily the individual it can best be tackled within the context of a specific social framework.

The lack of incentives seems at one time to have been considered almost the crucial problem in any attempts at economic development. It is possibly because of this past over-emphasis that there is today some reaction to this approach. The dust has not quite settled yet, but it might be possible to look at this problem, a little more soberly, as follows.

It may be assumed that the desire for higher incomes is general, but this desire, when analysed from the point of view of the individual, has to be referred to the social context of the individual's activities. The effects on incentives of the social context can be seen very clearly and quite easily in almost every colonial territory by comparing a cash-crop growing group, to a subsistence group within the same administrative boundaries: the incentives to production for an individual in the first group, who has joined a marketing system which puts him in economic contact with the whole outside world, have to be discussed on western lines; the incentives for an individual in the second group, who may not be far away geographically but for whom the world markets and their products are playing a fairly small part in life, may be of a kind quite baffling to a western economist.

Nevertheless, whatever the social context, the reasons for wanting a higher income remain basically similar:

The desire may be for access to more consumption goods, for 'a higher standard of living'.

The desire may be for greater wealth, either for reasons of prestige or in view of possible postponed consumption.

There may be an occasional desire, or need, for cash either for settling a debt—such as a capitation tax—or for some once-for-all acquisition, of the marriage fee or cattle purchase type.

The enjoyment of the fruits of an increased income, on the other hand, will usually be possible only within the society of which the individual is part. If, therefore, such income can only be earned away from that society, a system of labour migration will tend to arise: either periodical, as in the case of mining employees from regions too poor to provide a living, or involving only a few journeys in a life-time—sometimes only one—for the purpose of 'making his sum', as in the case of the young people from regions more fertile than in the previous case, but on the whole still of the subsistence economy type.[1] In such cases each individual has to strike some balance between his desire for cash and his need (which on the whole tends to be more important) for a normal life in his accustomed surroundings.

In the cases in which cash may be gained without migration, through the sale of local products on the local markets, the possibility of earning additional amounts can only become an incentive to further exertions when such amounts are large enough to break through the barrier of the indivisibilities of consumption or of individual investment. It is true, as Professor R. Firth has pointed out, that people adopt very easily new consumption patterns so that a Stone Age system of production might be combined with a western-type pattern of consumption. But western goods are adapted not only to western tastes but also to western standards of living, which imply much higher cash incomes than are the case in most of the colonial territories. An additional cash income of a few shillings a year would make little difference to the pattern of consumption or investment of an individual whose local system of exchange can provide him with practically all his normal necessities but whose desire for outside, cash goods such as a bicycle could only be met through a much bigger jump in income than the one within sight[2].

[1] Cf. J. Rouch (of the Musée de l'Homme, Paris) in his forthcoming publication on migration from the Niger province.
[2] Cf. F. Chalmers Wright: *African Consumers in Nyasaland and Tanganyika*.

It might be tentatively concluded that incentives could be at least as fruitfully discussed as being the *result* of obvious possibilities, within a given social context, of appreciably higher earnings than as the causes thereof.

MODERN TECHNIQUES NOT ADJUSTED TO LOCAL CONDITIONS

The modern techniques of production have been developed slowly in societies with specific social and economic networks of relationships by which they have been influenced and which in turn they have acted upon. The present complex of western production techniques is thus intricately bound up with the present western social and economic framework, including as a most important factor the level of income and capitalization.

In agriculture, techniques have been based on experiments carried out over centuries under conditions of temperature, rainfall and soils specific to the temperate climates. It is becoming more and more obvious that the type of farming thus evolved cannot be automatically introduced into the tropics. The contribution in knowledge and techniques which it can make to tropical agriculture will be less that of detailed farming practices than of methods of agricultural research and experimentation.

Western farming provides an essential basis from which to tackle the scientific, technical and economic problems of tropical farming; but post-war experience has proved conclusively the dangers of going beyond that. From the Atlantic to the Indian Ocean, Africa is dotted with the costly remains of attempts at the wholesale transplantation of agricultural techniques developed in temperate climates.

The close integration of western agriculture into the general western economic system has furthermore led to the development of industrial equipment able to cope with the specific problems of farming in the western communities. The high-labour-cost machine-intensive western agriculture has thus established techniques which involve complex types of equipment. There is sometimes a tendency to assume that the difficulty of using such equipment in the colonies is due to the low level of skills of the persons in charge. This is only partly true, as such skills can be fairly easily acquired, and the evidence derived from the rapid spread of mechanized vehicles and of the small repair shops for them shows that the problem is comparatively easily solved. The basic difficulty in the use of such equipment is the need for the costly stocking of large supplies of spare parts per unit of equipment in use.

The solution to this problem could be a large-scale expansion of the use of equipment, which would lower the proportion of spare parts per unit to be stocked; a speeding-up of the transport facilities from the main manufacturing centres, which would enable fresh stocks to be delivered more quickly; or the possibility of local manufacturing of spares. A different and possibly much better solution would be the design of implements specific to the economic conditions in the colonies. The main aim of such designs should be to ensure that most of the spare parts needed could be fairly easily manufactured within an industrially rudimentary economy.

Outside agriculture the problems raised by techniques and equipment geared to the western type of economy are less acute, both because they affect a fairly small proportion of the economy and because in many cases, such as mining, large-scale public works projects, power production and certain types of industrial undertakings, equipment tends to have a longer life, with spare parts being a smaller problem, and the production units are less affected by climatic differences than in the case of agriculture. In addition, there has been a much longer experience in the manufacturing world of coping with difficulties of climate and isolation in connection with such equipment.

THE BURDEN OF INCOME AND OUTPUT DISPARITIES

The differences in output and income per head between the colonial territories and the western societies also cause certain problems of adaptation. Some of these problems are connected with the already mentioned fact that the existing equilibrium between type of equipment and labour costs has been established on the basis of conditions in the west. But theories have been put forward attributing certain more fundamental effects to these differences. The argument is that the lower income prevalent in undeveloped countries, combined with the tendency towards consumptions imitative of western patterns, can only lead to a position of very low group investment (the 'Duesenberry' effect). This theory might be an over-simplification of the problems of investment in such societies. Data are difficult to get, not least because of the difficulty of defining investment as opposed to consumption under such circumstances. But if capital investment is looked at from the point of view of the creation of new productive capacity, a low proportion (as compared to the western communities) of total incomes privately invested might be more than made up for by the high productive yields of such investments. From the point of view of colonial development aggregate future yields (not percentage of present income) may be a better measure of the contribution of investments to the local economies and would certainly make more sense when priority decisions must be taken in economic policy.

An additional aspect of the difference in income per head between the colonial territories and the western communities of some significance today is the creation of a class of people whose output is related to the output levels within the local economies but whose income is determined by the income levels within the western economies. This applies especially to the people whose skills make them an internationally exchangeable commodity and whose basic remuneration is therefore at an internationally set level—such as administrators, technicians and similar salaried occupational classes. In order to attract foreigners to jobs in the colonial communities it is in fact necessary to pay them premiums over and above what they would receive in similar jobs in their own countries.

Attempts to insulate the colonial territories from these international levels of costs by the device of fairly low basic salaries and of high 'expatriate' allowances, leading to international-type payments only for the 'expatriates', tend to break down due to the emotions engendered by the social advantages which such differences create for a minority group within the community. As a result the income of all skilled groups in the colonies has been pushed up and the income differential between them and the average population is thus much higher than in the western communities not only because of a comparatively lower average income for the unskilled population but also because of a comparatively higher payment for skills. The cost of such skills to the colonies is thus disproportionately high and will tend to remain so until there are sufficient local technicians to cover local needs.

How long it will take after that point has been reached before these differentials will begin to resemble those in the western communities is difficult to say, especially as the western socio-economic structure is itself continuously changing. The lessening of the gap will tend to be slow if left to a raising of the general average income alone. A direct lowering of the salaries, fees and similar incomes of the skilled groups could hardly be envisaged. A fairly rapid upward adjustment of the incomes of the lower-paid groups, helped possibly by inflationary movements which would diminish the real income of the skilled groups, might have to be relied upon to bring about a more rapid diminution of the income differential. Meanwhile this peculiar version of a 'dual' type of economy will continue to impose a heavy economic and possibly also social strain on the colonial societies.

CHAPTER 3

Obstacles to Economic Planning in the Colonies

OVERBURDENED ADMINISTRATIONS UNACCUSTOMED TO PLANNING

THE analysis of the social and economic background of a community and of the means modern techniques have made available for its economic growth may indicate the problems of development such a community has to face and how it might be able to solve them; but planning such development involves two further essential ingredients: the determination to plan, and a planning machinery.

In the colonial territories the determination to plan has usually been fostered from the centre; the machineries for detailed planning, on the other hand, have often (especially in the case of the British territories) been set up within each territory by the territorial administrations concerned and have therefore been intimately connected with the structure and the problems of each of these administrations. Such planning machineries have to include two main kinds of specialists.

First of all, there must be people who are closely connected with, and personally aware of, the problems to be tackled and of the means available for tackling them. These problems are of many different kinds but may be broadly arranged into two groups.

The most straightforward, at least in the majority of cases, are the problems which may be called *technical*, in the sense that they are amenable to techniques developed within the framework of a certain existing body of knowledge and experience. Communications and public works generally, medical and veterinary treatment, are among the items which can be dealt with on the firm foundation of such 'technical' disciplines. Certain problems of law whose solution can facilitate economic growth, such as registration of property rights, as well as some economic problems, may be equally included among this technical group.

The *non-technical* problems, which roughly include most of the economic-social-political group of problems, present, on the other hand, difficulties whose solution is never final and which a technically biased planning machinery would seldom be able to cope with and often may not even be able to grasp. They form a shifting, protean-like mass and it is only possible to go so far in attempts to give that mass a definite shape and a definite direction unless methods of coercion are employed which are repugnant to a non-totalitarian tradition. The main reason for this difficulty is that the non-technical problems are at least as much subjective as objective. They can therefore only be dealt with after convincing the community that they are important, that they must be dealt with, and that their best solution is that put forward by the planners.

Secondly, and whatever the planning sphere or the proportion of technical and of non-technical problems within it, it is not sufficient that the planning machinery should include the experts appropriate to the various fields to be included in a plan: it must also include people knowledgeable in the processes of planning as such. The processes of planning have themselves their purely technical as well as their non-technical or 'committee' aspects, and both must somehow be taken care of for the successful drafting and implementation of a plan.

The territorial administrations have not found it easy to cope satisfactorily with the problem of setting up planning machineries. Some of the reasons have been connected with staffing problems, some with problems of organization, and some with the difficulties of adjustment to rapidly changing economic, technical and political situations. It would be difficult to make a complete analysis of the situation confronting the administrations, though an attempt at a survey of some of the more detailed problems of planning and of the administrative measures to deal with them will be made in Chapter 5. But there are certain problems of a more general character, which may be indicated here.

The most obvious among such problems has been the *shortage of staff*, both technical and administrative. This shortage has been, no doubt, the result of a general, world-wide, post-war situation, but it has been of differing intensities in the various territories, and in some it has tended to last much longer than in others. In the British territories the position in East Africa has thus on the whole been better than in West Africa. One possible explanation might be the larger reservoir of trained population in East Africa, drawn from comparatively larger European and Asiatic populations whose level of general education is higher than that of the average African population. The Belgian Congo is in a similar position in this respect.

Another reason for this shortage might be the reluctance of new recruits to go to countries which are at a stage of rapid political change. The general uncertainty about future status and conditions of service for expatriate members of the administrations undergoing rapid nationalization is very unsettling. The British system whereby each territory in which a civil servant works is responsible for part of his pension may in addition have influenced the more senior civil servants in their desire to move towards territories where possible defaults in payments seem less likely. The recent creation of an integrated British overseas civil service should help in lessening these uncertainties in the British territories.

A possibly less obvious but at least as important problem has been the tendency towards rapid transfers of staff as between jobs and as between territories. The disadvantage of such a system from the point of view of the continuity of development policies had already been pointed out in the British context in pre-war reports and has been re-emphasized by the West India Royal Commission.[1]

Looked at from the point of view of the needs of development planning, the staffing and organizational problems within the administrations go indeed much deeper. The colonial administrations seem to have been conceived of so far as a body of 'specialists' in colonial problems. As such they have been largely separated from other administrative departments in the metropolitan countries, though many of the problems to be dealt with in the colonies would fall much more neatly within the purview of, say, a Ministry of Health or a Ministry of Education. These 'colonial specialists' have, on the other hand, been expected to give proof of extraordinary diversity of knowledge and interests *within* the colonial framework, and to be able to cope with all the problems of administration in widely differing territories. This conception has, of course, been closely connected with the 'District Officer' or the 'Commandant du Cercle' system of administration. This system involves a large amount of delegation of power and authority to individuals each of whom has to deal with a separate area whose administrative problems cover a wide range, but are on the whole fairly rudimentary. On the understanding that the qualities of character and initiative of each officer are of the highest, this has possibly been both the cheapest and the most efficient system of administration, at least as long as what was wanted was peace, order and, generally speaking, a 'holding of the fort'. But for development planning, which involves the need for staff specialized not in 'colonial' problems but in each of the specific fields of planning within a specific territory, such decentralization is not of great help.

[1] Cf. *Cmd 6607*, chap. 5, para. 24.

The tendency therefore has been for administrations to rely heavily for their detailed planning on the few members of staff at headquarters. These tended to be especially the senior members of the technical departments within each territory, such as the medical, the agricultural, the public works, or the education departments (themselves staffed by frequent transfers between often dissimilar territories). The non-specialist administrative staff was then used chiefly for co-ordinating duties. Specialist departments throughout the world, even when not badly understaffed as has usually been the case in the colonies, tend to deal with problems not as part of a common endeavour but as each department's own separate sphere of activity. Among the most difficult problems of colonial planning has been that of finding means of co-operation between such departments.

The administrative background to planning, and this applies especially but not exclusively to the British territories, has thus been the dual one of a geographically decentralized regional or district administration involving a staff of self-sufficing and isolated non-specialists and of specialized, but also isolated, departments at the centre. This tendency of working in isolation both in the field and at headquarters has been further strengthened—almost paradoxically—by the already mentioned rapid transfers between departments and jobs. A continuing interest by an individual in the affairs of a department of which he used to be a member can be very easily misinterpreted as an attempt at criticizing colleagues now working in it. Under such circumstances 'the right man in the right place' has as its corollary 'the man in the place is the only right man'. This has tended to give rise to a great deal of touchiness in administrative discussions and is another reason why planning, especially at first, has often not gone beyond a summary of departmental plans.

As for the people whom the planning is supposed to affect, seldom have any means been found of taking them into effective consultation, let alone partnership. In the administration's relations with the population the situation has been especially complicated by the rather delicate personal position of the 'expatriate' or 'overseas' members. Each expatriate colonial civil servant, besides representing the rule of law, is also, in reality as well as emotionally, an 'envoy' of his home country. This means that his behaviour (again especially but not exclusively in the British territories) has tended on the whole to be the dignified one both of a ruler and of an ambassador, leading to a certain aloofness from the population at large. The differences in customs, in language and in material and educational backgrounds between him and the population further strengthen this aloofness. The only type of emotional relation which has, on the whole, been approved of within this system is that often quoted of guardians and wards. Guardians are notoriously unable, as many have pointed out, to understand the needs and the emotional processes of their wards.

As a result of this triad of functions—of ruler, envoy and civil servant—any uninvited criticisms or any attacks against the actions of an official made from outside the administration tend to be taken at the same time as attacks against the rule of law, against the sovereign the official 'represents', and against a body which, according to the western parliamentary system, must not be criticized directly—and therefore as a mixture of subversion, of *lèse majesté*, and of a breach of good manners. Hence the intense and honest distress and disgust of administrators at any such attacks in the past and the willingness to 'call out the legions'. Hence also the growing pleasure and relief, after initial moments of grave doubts, of many administrators at increasing political representation and at the assumption of executive and policy-making duties by elected members of the public, who are thus providing both a political shield and a link between the population and the civil service.

But these political shields and these links have been slow in coming, and in most colonial territories development plans have been drawn up and implemented while they were still only being hammered into shape. It is especially their functions as links whose absence has been most felt in planning. Political bodies are not only the best fitted to interpret the population's views, feelings and desires, but also best able to give an often necessary lead. Without such interpretation and without the possibility of such a lead, planning will seldom be able to gear the population to a common effort for development. Purely administrative planning has therefore to be, as a whole, limited to those fields which have always been tacitly accepted within each respective community as belonging to the sphere of administration proper, and which are restricted mostly to the solution of technical problems. To request a civil service which does not have a political system to lean upon to go beyond that would not only be unfair, it would also impose upon it a burden under which it might well break down.

ECONOMIC ARTIFICIALITY OF ADMINISTRATIVE UNITS

The population in most of the colonies has a low average density and, with few exceptions, tends to coagulate in discrete groups.

OBSTACLES TO ECONOMIC PLANNING

Many of the colonial territories are thus 'under-populated' in the absolute sense that they contain areas without population and in which people could make a living at a standard not very different from that in existence elsewhere in the territory. There are, in other words, empty and potentially productive lands. In certain cases migrant populations may change the size and shape of the population pockets from year to year or even from season to season, but such migrant populations (not to be confused with migrant labour) form a small and diminishing proportion of the total populations. The population concentrations tend, in other words, to be geographically fairly permanent.

Such concentrations of population need not have a homogeneous aspect socially or economically. Tribes or nations may live in close proximity or even intermingled; different languages may be used indiscriminately in the same population group; religious beliefs and practices, systems of inheritance, traditional administrative customs, may all be widely different within the group. This raises a number of problems of local adjustments, creates social tensions and may introduce obstacles to economic development, but their very diversity makes it necessary to discuss such local problems in their actual context, group by group. In certain ways these strains and stresses, even when powerful enough to raise the spectre of a possibly explosive disintegration, tend to bring further distinguishing features to each separate population group, to individuate it, to give it a personality different from that of other, geographically separate groups. Such a contiguous population group, however diverse its constituents, cannot, as far as its economic life is concerned, be easily unscrambled or even realistically discussed on the basis of its constituent elements taken in isolation. Problems of economic development, however much local diversities might complicate them, have thus to be studied and solved on a geographical group basis.

The population groups can vary considerably from a number of points of view. Their size may range from a few thousand people to an appreciable number of millions. They may be socially homogeneous and stable, belonging to one single tribe or nation; or they may be a continuously changing mixture, as is especially the case in an economically very active community with a great power of attraction for neighbouring groupings. They may be comparatively isolated; or they may be in geographical proximity to other groups. They may belong to a subsistence type of economy which will strengthen their isolation; or be at various stages of specialization which will tend to bring them nearer to other groups, not necessarily neighbouring ones.

The groups may thus vary from the hundreds of small communities of Tanganyika, each one self-sufficient within its subsistence economy, to the cash-crop communities of Uganda, Nigeria or French Senegal, which run to millions and have become fairly highly specialized. There seems, indeed, to be a fairly close correlation in these territories between group size on the one hand, and specialization and hence dependence upon the outside world on the other. The reverse process—of the *broadening* of the range of local productive activities at the more advanced technical levels made possible by contacts with the outside world—can only come about after specialization, group size and average income have all progressed sufficiently. Attempts at short cuts towards diversification have often led to a wasteful employment of available resources.

Each one of these population groups has had to establish its own connections with the complementary economies overseas from which it can draw its cash income and its supplies of manufactured goods and of technical knowledge. This need for communications has determined the broad lines of development for all the colonial territories. The population groups which have had access to cheap methods of transport, especially the sea, have not only been the first to establish an active internal exchange economy arising from their international trade and thus to take the first steps towards specialization both on an internal and on an international basis, but have also been in the privileged position of having a larger choice of cash products for export, as bulk has been less of a drawback. Population groups which have not had such an advantage have had to base their economic development on products of higher value per unit of bulk, and thus on a narrower range.

The connections once established and the process of specialization begun, the tendency for the specializing group to enlarge itself by the integration of neighbouring groups into its own exchange economy has been an important feature of economic and social development throughout the colonies. Again, costs of transport have been important and groups beyond a certain distance from the specialized group have been able to enter only in partial relationships with it through the exchange of non-bulky goods or of economic products or factors whose transport is cheap, such as cattle on the hoof or migrant labour.

Such natural economic relations tend to appear unsatisfactory to a political administration whose tendency, based on ideas developed in a western context, is to treat every individual and every community within the administrative boundaries on a footing of equality without regard to its geographical location. This can lead to awkward situations, especially as administrative divisions in the colonies often have little in common with the natural geographical population groups. There is every conceivable combination of administrative boundaries and population groupings; a number of independent groupings might exist within the same boundaries; one group might be split up between two or more administrative territories; or territorial boundaries and population groups might overlap in different proportions for any of the groups within a territory. The problem is not peculiar to colonial territories but is especially widespread there, and time has been too short to allow of that merging of groups within an administrative boundary which gives so many of the historically more ancient administrative entities their unity in diversity. An extreme example of the tendency to artificial unification is the attempt by the French authorities in the fairly recent past of developing communications, especially in French West and Equatorial Africa, on the principle that transport costs to the harbours for export goods should be roughly equivalent whatever the distance they might have to travel. The transport costs of a ton of groundnuts should, in accordance with this conception, have been roughly the same whether they had to travel a few miles from the neighbourhood of Dakar or have come right across from the Sudan. In compact western economies the equation of transport costs whatever the distance is of course a well-known commercial practice in connection with the majority of consumption goods, and it applies now and again even to certain among the basic raw materials, such as steel. The economic reasons in favour of such an arrangement, which may be strong within the western economies though often debatable even under such circumstances, are weak when applied to colonial territories in which there is no continuous population forming one homogeneous geographical unit but only artificial administrative areas containing discrete population pockets with wide empty gaps between.

If administrative practice is to emulate commercial policies it should, in any case, not transform a tenet of *western* commercial policy into one of colonial administrative practice. The colonial commercial policies tend to be fairly consistent in dealing, in the case both of imported goods sold on the local markets and of purchases of local products for export, strictly on a c.i.f. basis. No valid economic reason and only rather weak political or other non-economic reasons can be put forward for neglecting the c.i.f. factor in the case of public expenditure on development projects.

There is, of course, no reason to accept the existence of such economically isolated population groups as a permanent feature. Their integration into wider units, which need not coincide with existing administrative units, is continually taking place either through administrative measures or through economic or other developments independent of administrative action.

CHAPTER 4

Policies for Development

INTRODUCTION OF NEW TECHNIQUES:
SMALL-SCALE PRODUCTION

EXCEPTIONAL individuals who can invent entirely new and better ways of production or accumulation—or speculation—are by definition few. What is within the reach of everybody are small improvements. These are not easy in a society which, as is the case with most of the colonial societies, has been built not for progress but for survival and hence for stability. Even when such a community has become 'growth-conscious' the existing basis of local activities is usually much too narrow to allow sufficient scope for the type of economic growth which is based on improving processes already in existence within the community. Such growth could only become effective at a much later stage of economic development. Economic growth must therefore be based on the imitation of improvements brought in from outside. When such outside improvements have been introduced and their earning possibilities have become clear, they spread quickly throughout the group. Cash crops have thus been widely and willingly taken up, more often than not without any 'official' efforts or backing; and practically all viable local industries (which have usually also been the result of private initiatives) have developed from the imitation of a newly introduced type of industrial plant. Future developments, to be sufficiently rapid, will have to continue to be based on such imitative actions. Hence there is pressing need for a flow from outside of new techniques, skills and processes, including the introduction of new types of products, agricultural as well as industrial, which can suit local conditions. Purely economically speaking, the colonies which have opened their doors wide to immigration from technically more advanced communities, such as some of the British colonies in East and Central Africa, the Belgian Congo and some of the French territories, have therefore a much better chance for a rapid and healthy development of their resources than those which restrict the inflow and attempt a premature policy of self-sufficiency in matters of entrepreneurship and skilled man-power.

There is an important qualification for the widespread introduction of such new techniques: they must involve equipment suited to the capital structure within the community. The equipment must, in other words, either be sufficiently cheap, like the pressure-sprayers against fruit-crop pests, to be within financial reach of potential users, or it must have, like the motor lorries, quick returns sufficiently high to enable a rapid repayment of money borrowed for its purchase or of hire-purchase instalments. Available resources can allow only of low investments per head of worker.

At the same time, such new introductions should not involve improvements of too minute a character, e.g. of the often advocated 'better hoe' variety. Such improvements tend to be rejected, the difficulties of adjusting life-long skills in the use of one implement more than making up for the possible, but not always very obvious, better future results from the new version.

The colonial labour problems have not as a whole yet reached the stage of time-and-motion studies. The change which seems successful both in its acceptance by the population and in results is typified by the replacement, for heavy agricultural work, of the hoe with the bullock-drawn plough.

INTRODUCTION OF NEW TECHNIQUES: LARGE-SCALE PRODUCTION

Though the approach along the lines of small-scale production has shown good results in most cases and is applicable to the majority of activities in the colonies, it cannot be successfully used in every single case. Obvious exceptions are the type of public works such as harbours, railways, roads and power production, where efficiency both in construction and in running is closely connected with high capital investments and with advanced technical standards and design. Obvious exceptions also are the mines. This has led to the conclusion that economic development in the colonies may be split along certain 'natural' lines, namely: public works; mines and 'modern' industries; and agriculture. Such a division is unfortunate, as it tends to give the impression that each of these three main groups may be dealt with independently of the other two. Especially unfortunate is the severance of the agricultural sector from the other two.

The higher concentration of capital which public works, mines and industries require and their employment of modern machinery and of technically skilled labour gives the impression that it is such activities which involve a real technical advance and hence lead to economic development *par excellence*; but in communities in which most of the population is engaged either in agricultural pursuits or in pursuits closely connected with agriculture, the activities included under public works, industries and, from certain aspects, even mining must be placed squarely within the context of agricultural development. It is not only unrealistic in such cases but it is directly harmful to economic development to look on agriculture as an infantile complaint and to concentrate all efforts on outgrowing it.

An analysis of possible alternative approaches towards the capital-intensive economic activities may make the problem a little clearer.

Public Works. The constructional activities of the administration, here dumped under 'public works', cover a wide range and include much which does not come directly under economic development as usually understood, such as schools, hospitals and housing. The main 'economic' public works may be classified under communications, water and power supplies, with communications usually by far the most important. (Water and power supplies are best dealt with in connection with agriculture and industries.)

The economic rôle of communications in the colonies is all-pervasive. Certain of its aspects have been dealt with in the previous chapter under 'Economic Artificiality of Administrative Units', and others will be dealt with in more detail in the discussion on individual priorities in Chapter 15. What may be said here, in summary, is that communications can either be provided to meet existing transport needs or can be used to encourage development in a stagnant but potentially active region. In either case their main functions will be to deal, first, with agricultural goods whether for local consumption or for export, and, secondly, with consumption goods, most of them imported, for the use mainly of the agricultural populations.

Agricultural activities, and the needs of the farming population, are thus the main economic justifications for colonial communications, and a sound communications system will have to be built on the basis of a main-road network to connect the principal agricultural regions with the outside world, and of a feeder-road system to connect individual population groups with the main network.

The main exception to this generalization seems to be provided by the transport needs of the mining centres, whose own position in the colonial economies will be roughly outlined below.

Mining. The contribution of mining to colonial development can be direct, through payments to the colonies' budgets, either in the form of royalties or of various types of taxes. Or it can be indirect, through the employment of local labour, the provision of facilities which can be profitably used by other members of the community and the creation of a market for increased, or even for entirely new, types of production within the community. These indirect contributions will vary from case to case, from nil, as exemplified until recently by the bauxite mining on the shores of French Guinea, to the cases of the Belgian Congo or of Northern Rhodesia, where the whole economic development has been induced by mining activities.

But even in these latter cases mining on its own can in most instances only take the economic development of the group up to a certain point. Even though its cash contribution to the economy can be much greater than anything envisaged before, it will usually employ directly only a small percentage of the population, and it can carry only so much of the rest of the population towards an increasing standard of living. To ensure a continuous increase in the output of the colony will sooner or later necessitate a higher productivity from the majority of the population who for an appreciable time to come will continue to be the farmers. One of the most important contributions that mining can make to a colony's development is thus to facilitate its agricultural development, through the creation of links with the outside world as well as through the provision of additional capital to the community.

Industries. The present approach to industrial development, especially when governments become interested in fostering it, could be classified into an 'imports list' and an 'exports list' type.

In the imports-list type the existence of a potential local market for any one product is deduced after an inspection of the quantity of various goods imported.[1] The economics of local production for each commodity which has already a sufficiently large local market is then analysed in terms of the optimum size of the production units, the availability of local resources in raw materials and labour, and the potential saving in transport costs as compared to imports.

In the exports-list type the exports of raw materials are investigated to discover the economic possibilities of local processing for export, especially in connection with bulk saving or with the possibility of making use of certain additional and otherwise unused, or less profitably used, local resources such as labour or cheap power.

[1] Cf. W. A. Lewis: *Report on Industrialization and the Gold Coast,* 1953.

Both these approaches are useful within their limits, but these limits when soberly appraised are found to be exceedingly narrow.[1] Even on their own premises such approaches tend to stop short of a logical conclusion. Thus, in the case of the imports-list approach they seldom have the necessary information or the courage to take into account the possibilities of an expansion of the market due both to the cheapening of the product and to its more ready and stable availability. But the main objection to these approaches is of a more fundamental kind: they do not make use of the possibilities of growth inherent in an economic system.

These possibilities of growth are especially connected with the increasing needs for the tools of production. Manufactured consumption goods will, as a whole, be uneconomic to produce locally except in the comparatively few instances fulfilling the conditions enumerated when discussing the imports-list approach. Throughout most of the colonial territories the greatly improved harbour facilities and internal systems of communications tend to make the price differentials due to transport costs on manufactured goods comparatively small and, with an exiguous local market, the possibilities of competing against mass manufactures cannot be very optimistically viewed. But in the case of tools a very important additional consideration comes in.

Temporary shortages of this or that consumption good, though possibly inconvenient, rarely lead to hardships. There is both a wide range of substitutes and a possibility of postponed consumption. A broken-down tool for which there is no immediate replacement or repair facilities will, on the other hand, lead to an appreciable loss of income, especially in an agricultural community with its seasonal outputs and perishable products. Though the new harbours and inland communications have cheapened transport, distances from the manufacturing centres overseas are still great and so are the delays in the arrival of ordered goods; and the holding of large stocks of spares to meet all possible emergencies is highly uneconomic, both because of the capital locked up and because of the risk of being left with unsaleable goods. As the reliance of agriculture on more and more complicated machinery and implements is increasing—today still limiting itself mainly to the means of transport, from carrier bicycles to heavy lorries for agricultural products, but beginning to

[1] The Lewis Report estimated possible additional employment in the Gold Coast, in industries developed along these lines, at a maximum of 2,000 a year in the near future, a maximum which is very far from having been reached. The natural population increase in the Gold Coast (now Ghana) is probably in the region of 70,000 a year.

spread also into working implements—the need for local workshops and manufactures to keep this machinery going is also increasing. Most of the 'industrial' workers throughout the colonies are connected with the vehicle repair shops which help to keep agricultural goods moving. Future industrialization may well be healthiest and most dynamic if it were to develop in continuing and close contact with the farmers' needs for tools.

BALANCED GROWTH AND EXTERNAL ECONOMIES

There have been certain other approaches, from a rather different angle, to the problems of economic growth in low-income territories. These approaches are related especially to non-agricultural activities —though in certain cases they can also be extended to agriculture— and have been variously and sometimes rather vaguely known under such names as balanced growth, organic growth, or *grand ensemble*. They have usually been connected with the concepts of external economies or of social net products. Before analysing these types of approach it might be useful to attempt to clear up some confusion which seems to exist in the use of the term 'external economies'.

In the case of internal economies it is clear that the economy arises from changes within the firm and results in benefits to the firm. The firm is the only point of reference and the world outside it has little relevance in this context.

External economies, on the other hand, can only be understood, by definition, as the result of an inter-action between a firm and the outside world. With two points of reference there immediately appear certain possibilities of variation.

A *first type* of external economies are those which arise from changes in the outside world and which result in benefits to the firm. This seems to have been the case Marshall had in mind in the passage in which he classified economies of growth into internal and external. 'We may divide the economies arising from an increase in the scale of production of any kind of goods into two classes—firstly, those dependent upon the general development of the industry; and secondly, those dependent upon the resources of the individual houses of business engaged in it, on their organization, and the efficiency of their management. We may call the former *external economies* and the latter *internal economies*.'[1] Marshall obviously meant *external* and *internal* to be taken as relative to the firm.

[1] A. Marshall, *Principles of Economics*, 8th ed., 1946, p. 266.

A *second type* of external economies are those which arise from changes within a firm and which result in benefits to the outside world. This seems to be the case most usually discussed today under the designation of the social net product of a firm's activities, and it is the case which is often relevant in discussions of the problems of growth of undeveloped countries.

A *third type* of economies which have also been called external arises from the multiple relations and cross-relations between an unstated number of firms or of groups of firms in an expanding economy. It is this third type of economies which Marshall probably had in mind when he discussed the 'correlated branches of industry which mutually assist one another'. 'Meanwhile an increase in the aggregate scale of production of course increases those economies which do not directly depend on the size of individual houses of business. The most important of these result from the growth of correlated branches of industry which mutually assist one another, perhaps being concentrated in the same localities, but, anyhow, availing themselves of the modern facilities for communication offered by steam transport, by the telegraph, and by the printing press.'[1] In the rest of the text Marshall exemplified but did not define his 'correlated branches of industry'. He seems to have had in mind both a vertical and a horizontal 'correlation'.

Professor Young restated Marshall's definition of this type of 'external' economies: 'Consider, for example, Alfred Marshall's fruitful distinction between the internal productive economies which a particular firm is able to secure as the growth of the market permits it to enlarge the scale of its operations and the economies external to the individual firm which show themselves only in changes of the organization of the industry as a whole.'[2]

These 'external' economies as defined by Marshall and restated by Professor Young seem in fact to be *industry-internal* economies, and their quality of being external to any one individual firm, though true, is not really relevant to their economic analysis. In the same way in which a discussion of firm-internal economies is concerned with the pattern of relationships within a firm, what is of interest in a discussion of industry-internal economies is the pattern of relationships within an industry—using 'industry' in its undifferentiated sense, as a complex of varied industrial operations. 'In recapitulation of these variations on a theme [the 'division of labour' theme] from

[1] Ibid., p. 317.
[2] Allyn Young: 'Increasing Returns and Economic Progress', *Economic Journal*, December 1928, p. 527.

Adam Smith, there are two parts to be stressed. First, the mechanism of increasing returns is not to be discerned adequately by observing the effects of variations in the size of an individual firm or of an industry, for the progressive division and specialization of industries is an essential part of a process by which industrial returns are realized. What is required is that industrial operations be seen as an interrelated whole.'[1]

It is these 'industry-internal' economies within an 'interrelated whole' which are the type of 'external' economies most directly relevant to the balanced growth and the *grand ensemble* approaches to the economic development of low-income territories. The continued use of the (rather inappropriate) definition of 'external' for these economies is probably due to the fact that the terminological implications of the switch in perspective from the 'firm' to the 'industry' as the centre of interest, already implied in the second of the passages from Marshall quoted above and fully developed by Professor Young, were relatively unimportant in the context of their main interests. A greater clarity may be desirable in connection with present-day discussions of the problems of growth in undeveloped countries.

A further ambiguity in the discussions on the problems of development, not unconnected with the confusion between firm-external and industry-internal economies, has been introduced by some confusion between the external economies of a firm and the causes of these economies. This has led to a rather loose classification of external economies into vertical and horizontal.

A firm may benefit from external economies only in access to more advantageous inputs or in a better market for its outputs. External economies enjoyed by a firm can therefore only be of a vertical type. (A similar reasoning applies to the external economies created by a firm.) But these external economies may be the result of either a horizontal or a vertical industrial change, and quite often of a combination of both. A horizontal expansion might thus create a larger pool of labour and management, enabling an individual firm to have access to a better selection of skills, and the advantages of a vertical expansion are even more direct and obvious. The vertical expansion itself might, of course, result from a previous horizontal expansion which has provided the necessary conditions for the employment of factors working under conditions of indivisibility, and the horizontal expansion from better supplies or a larger demand due to vertical expansions.

[1] Ibid., p. 539.

The internal economies, on the other hand, whether firm- or industry-internal, *can* be both vertical and horizontal, the latter usually in connection with a horizontal reorganization.

The economies of growth and their significance for the economic development of a low-income community may now be discussed in the light of this new systematization.

The first case, that of external economies accruing to a firm and arising from the growth of the industry, is normally of little interest in the context of an undeveloped community in which each firm tends to fend for itself (though possibly with public subsidies) in an isolated, pioneer status. Even when the stage is reached in which an industry has been created, planners (whose activities are the main subject of this study) will seldom be interested in fostering further external economies for the sake of benefiting some individual firm.

The second case (which is very close to that of a social net product) of external economies resulting from the creation or the expansion of a firm and benefiting the industrial world outside the firm, has been much more successful in gripping the attention of both economists and administrators. The obvious (and already mentioned) example in colonial economics are the mines, which provide services, such as communications, open to other productive activities; a nucleus of people with technical and sometimes managerial skills usable in other enterprises; markets for local products; and a source of capital which sometimes has been the decisive factor in the economic development of the territory. Cheap sources of power, especially hydro-electric power, can have similar effects. But mines or hydro-electric power can only occur where there happen to be discoveries of mineral wealth or easily managed water-flows.

The search for a type of enterprise with similar external economies as the mines but which could be established wherever the need for it may be most acute has been one of the most cherished ambitions of people concerned with problems of development. It is not easy to discover any successful example of such an enterprise in any of the colonial territories with the possible, but terminologically doubtful, exception of such service-producing enterprises as harbours. The nearest approximation might be power-packages based on atomic processes, but this is still little more than theoretical speculation about the future. Nevertheless project after project from new roads or railways to various kinds of pioneer plants have been put forward in the expectation that they would provide external economies to other, existing or potential, activities.

The repeated losses incurred by many such projects, especially when undertaken with public funds or subsidies, have led to an awareness of the difficulties involved in setting up one single enterprise without the normal industrial background. The theoretical answer to this problem has been the *grand ensemble* or the balanced growth in which, in Professor Young's words, the industrial operations could be seen as an interrelated whole or in which, as in the more recent exposition by Mr Fleming, the plants 'would jointly yield a positive net product, even though individually none of them would do so'.[1] No such *grand ensemble* has yet been set up to enable some test of this theory, but its dangers are obvious: though it might have more chances of success than the many single enterprises set up with public funds throughout the colonies, its failure would involve the loss of much greater resources than any yet invested in individual industrial projects.

Similar from some points of view to the *grand ensemble* approach but less discussed recently in economic literature is the multi-purpose project. The example of such a project which most readily springs to mind is that carried out by the Tennessee Valley Authority. There has, in fact, been a plethora of similar projects dotted throughout the colonies, though their similarity with the basic principle of the TVA has usually been hidden to cursory glances because of their different backgrounds. The most popular attempts at such 'little TVAs' have been the mechanized agricultural projects, each one with a combination of aims as widely divergent as population resettlement, experimentation—with new crops, new agricultural methods and new systems of land tenure,—provision of large-scale supplies of cheap foods and, obviously, the introduction of mechanical and scientific techniques as yet unknown and untried in such surroundings. Economically speaking they have been failures in practically every instance. The reasons are not far to seek: the TVA project has been firmly based on a well-tried-out combination of known resources —water-power and phosphates for the production of super-phosphates—and on a large and ready supply of skills and of technical knowledge, whereas the mechanized agriculture projects in the colonies have been launched on faith into the unknown without any firm standby of any description.

[1] M. Fleming: 'External Economies and the Doctrine of Balanced Growth', *Economic Journal*, June 1955, pp. 244–5.

PART III
AN HISTORICAL OUTLINE

CHAPTER 5

The Growth of the Idea of Development Planning for Colonial Territories

THE approach to a policy of planning in the colonies has been fairly gradual; and whether the actual planning is done centrally by the metropolitan government or locally by the authorities within the respective colonial territory, the main impulse has almost always tended to come from the centre, from the metropolitan government concerned. There is little doubt that the policies of the metropolitan governments have influenced each other, though to varying extents. The most influential, on the whole, seems to have been the British policy, especially as far as French colonial thinking is concerned. But it would not be easy to give chapter and verse for these reciprocal influences: the process seems to have been one of individual influences on administrators, or of the spread of political views.

THE BRITISH EXPERIENCE: (A) CHANGES IN METROPOLITAN POLICIES

Treasury Grants and Colonial Loans. The British Government has always taken an interest in the economic viability of the colonial territories, and Treasury grants (amounting to £12 million between 1930 and 1940)[1] have been made to cover territorial budget deficits or extraordinary expenditure. In addition to the rather passive Treasury grants system of rescue measures, a more active method, that of colonial loans, has been used to foster economic development. Such loans have either been provided by direct advances from United Kingdom funds[2] or have been facilitated by a system of guarantees including arrangements (through the Colonial Stock Act) for entitling colonial loans issued on the London market to rank as trustee stock. But these loans have been connected

[1] *Cmd 6175*, para. 5.
[2] The British Government has remitted, under provisions made in the Act of 1940, a fairly large part of these loans, estimated at the time at some £11·3 million (*Cmd 6422*, para. 9) and since at about £10 million (*Cmd 9375*, para. 4).

with individual items of expenditure, for *ad hoc* purposes. They have involved no problems of integrated planning.

The Empire Marketing Board. The first approach to a policy of centrally guided economic development (though not of development plans) occurred in 1926 with the creation of the Empire Marketing Board, to assist the Secretary of State for Dominion Affairs in the administration of an *ad hoc* fund. The origin of the Board may be traced to the discussions which took place during the Imperial Economic Conference (the first of its kind) of 1923 and to the recommendations of the Imperial Economic Committee set up in 1925. Its purpose was to promote production throughout the Empire, including not only the colonial and trust territories but also the United Kingdom and the Dominions, through methods of research, facilities for marketing and more efficient systems of production, especially in the agricultural fields.

The 1929 Colonial Development Act. Additional impulses towards a conscious policy for the economic development of the Empire were given by the growing preoccupation of the UK Government with the problem of unemployment at home, especially after the onset of the world economic crisis. The Colonial Development Act of 1929, one of the first measures of the new Labour Government, empowered the Government to spend £1 million a year on colonial development and combined some of the aims of the Empire Marketing Board, especially in matters of research, with the techniques of Lloyd George's 1909 United Kingdom Road Development Fund.

'1. The Treasury, with the concurrence of the Secretary of State for the Colonies and on the recommendation of the committee to be appointed for the purpose of this Act, may make advances to the Government of any colony or of any territory to which this section applies, for the purposes of aiding and developing agriculture and industry in the colony or territory and thereby promoting commerce with or industry in the United Kingdom. . . .'[1]

Both the Labour Government, which brought in the Act, and the Opposition emphasized that additional employment in England was one of its hoped-for effects. Mr Thomas, who moved the Bill, said:

'. . . this Measure has been introduced on a Friday afternoon four weeks after I have taken office. This Measure has been introduced by a Labour Government, not only because we believe in

[1] *Colonial Development Act of 1929.*

GROWTH OF THE DEVELOPMENT PLANNING IDEA 59

Colonial Development and because it is urgent but because I think it will assist me in carrying out my ideas of dealing with unemployment.'[1]

Mr Amery on behalf of the Conservative Party had already given his full support to the Bill in the committee debate on Supply on April 30, 1929.[2] In discussing the Colonial Development Fund to be established under the Act, he said:

'I have no doubt that such a Fund, in which Ministers would be helped with the best expert advice available, administered on flexible lines, such as those which have so much facilitated the work of the Empire Marketing Board, can be made a most potent instrument for accelerating the general development of many regions of the colonial empire, and in doing so will contribute not only to the welfare of the inhabitants of the colonies concerned, but also, both directly in orders for the equipment of railways and other public works, and indirectly in the general expansion of trade, to the creation of much needed employment in this country.'

Nevertheless the debate which followed made it quite obvious that both the Government and the Opposition were fully aware that the contribution of the Colonial Development Act to the alleviation of unemployment in Britain at the time could only be insignificant. The actual increase in output in the colonial territories through the expenditure on development would obviously be slow in coming, whether it was in mining, where the interval between the undertaking of surveys and the beginning of exploitation had to be counted in years, or in agriculture and tropical products, where development was both chancy and long-drawn-out. The only relatively quick contribution would have been in terms of the demand for capital equipment for the public works contemplated, and this could only have amounted to a fraction of the total sums—of up to only £1 million a year—granted to the colonial empire as a whole, as these sums had to cover also the payment for the local labour and the local materials within the colonies.

It is difficult not to feel that the general willingness to approve of all measures which might help in relieving unemployment in the United Kingdom may have been used more as an argument in favour of undertaking within the colonial empire public works of whose

[1] *Hansard*, July 12, 1929, cols. 1299, 1300.
[2] Ibid., April 30, 1929, cols. 1412, 1413.

need most political leaders were becoming aware—the only real controversy between the Government and the Opposition concerning the Colonial Development Act seems to have been on who could claim to have thought of it first[1]—and that the actual contribution to a solution of the unemployment problem may well not have been of more than psychological importance.

Though the ultimate aim of the development of the colonial empire had thus been unambiguously stated to be that of helping the economy of the mother country, it is, furthermore, clear that the intention was not to 'exploit' the resources of the colonies—in the sense of 'robbing' them of the results of the labour of their populations or of their natural exhaustible wealth—for the profit of the United Kingdom, but to use the capital and technical resources of the United Kingdom to enable the economic development of territories whose economic backwardness and low productivity were felt to be due to a shortage of such resources. The assumption was naturally that, properly employed, the return to such resources for the United Kingdom would be at least as high as in possible alternative uses.

Under the Colonial Development Act of 1929 the British Government spent, over a period of eleven years, some £8·8 million in direct grants.[2]

The Moyne Commission and the 1940 Colonial Development and Welfare Act. The world depression and the drastic fall in the prices of agricultural commodities (and of raw materials generally), and especially in the demand for the luxury type of food products, such as cane sugar and tropical fruits, led to especially grave economic difficulties in the West Indies and to a series of troubles and riots. A Royal Commission was appointed in 1938 under Lord Moyne to investigate the basic problems in the West Indies and to suggest solutions. The outbreak of the war complicated the work of the Commission, especially by its effects on the facilities of movement for its members, but a summary of its report could nevertheless be presented to Parliament in 1940.[3] The Government decided, primarily as an act of faith and as an expression of its intentions, to transfer the main recommendations of the Royal Commission from their limited context of the West Indies to the whole of the Colonial Empire.[4] Mr MacDonald, in introducing the 1940 Colonial Develop-

[1] Cf. the issues of *Hansard* covering the debates on the Colonial Development Act.
[2] Cf. *Cmd 9375*, para. 2.
[3] *Cmd 6174*.
[4] *Cmd 6175*.

ment and Welfare Bill designed to implement the new policy based on the Moyne Report, emphasized that this implied a change in the official British approach to the problems of colonial development. On the Order for the Second Reading he said:

'There is, for instance, the existing Colonial Development Act. That Act is a most valuable Measure which has been on the Statute Book for the last ten years, but it is one which this Bill now seeks to supersede. Those who are familiar with the debates of 1929 will remember that even then the primary purpose of our legislation was not to help colonial development for its own sake, but in order to stimulate that development mostly to bring additional work to idle hands in this country. It was devised as part of our scheme to solve our own unemployment problem.

'In that respect, as in other respects, the Bill which we are discussing this afternoon breaks new ground. It establishes the duty of the taxpayers in this country to contribute directly, and for its own sake, towards the development in the widest sense of the word of the colonial peoples for whose good government the taxpayers of this country are ultimately responsible.'[1]

In his description of the 1929 Act Mr MacDonald was less than just to the spirit which moved not only his father and his father's colleagues but the whole of the House of Commons at that time. Nevertheless the new Act, whose name was significantly changed to the Colonial Development *and Welfare* Act, was certainly conceived in a much wider and warmer spirit. It was a challenge with almost Gallic *panache*, and even the obvious impossibility of fulfilling its implied promises does not detract from the sense of deep responsibility towards the British colonial territories which both the Act and the Debates evinced.

Wartime Retrenchment and the 1945 Colonial Development and Welfare Act. Very little was actually done to implement the Act except in the West Indies, which had been mainly responsible for the decision to initiate the Act and where an organization was set up under Sir Frank Stockdale to deal with the problems of the allocation of local as well as of Colonial Development and Welfare Fund resources for the purposes put forward in the Act. Some local attempts at planning the expenditure of possible Colonial Development and Welfare Fund allocations were undertaken and a certain

[1] *Hansard*, May 21, 1940, col. 45.

number of schemes were put forward and approved, but wartime shortages, not only of materials but also of administrative personnel, made of such attempts little more than theoretical exercises. From 1940 until 1945 only £2,860,000[1] were spent under an Act which had provided for a total possible expenditure of up to £5 million a year on development and welfare and up to £500,000 on research. Of this sum some £1,800,000 were spent in the West Indies, leaving just over £1 million for the rest of the whole of the colonial empire. It was therefore important to look again at the problem more realistically at the end of the war. With a victorious conclusion of the world conflict in sight, the 1945 Colonial Development and Welfare Act was passed increasing the total sums to be contributed by the United Kingdom to 'One hundred and twenty million pounds in the period of ten years ending with the thirty-first day of March, nineteen hundred and fifty-six'.[2]

Even though the sums to be made available were thus appreciably increased, being more than doubled in monetary terms, the possible contribution of such sums to the welfare needs of the colonial empire was more realistically appraised than in 1940. Colonel Stanley, Secretary of State for Colonial Affairs, gave the following warning in the debate on the Bill:

'I want to make it plain that this fund is not, is never intended to be, and never could be the sole and permanent support of all the social requirements of the whole of the colonial empire.'[3]

The Increasing Importance Attached to Planning. At the same time planning became a much more important feature of the approach to colonial development. This was due no doubt partly to the general wartime experience of the need for, and the effectiveness of, interdepartmental co-operation and partly to the results of the work of Sir Frank Stockdale's organization in the West Indies. What appeared to have been the very successful Russian and German experiments may also have semi-consciously permeated official thinking with a belief in the efficiency of long-range economic planning. The colonies, with their very much simpler economic structure and their apparent need for heavy public investment, may have seemed an ideal field for the application of ideas successfully developed by the administrations of the great totalitarian countries.

---

[1] *Hansard*, January 24, 1945, col. 2153.
[2] *Colonial Development and Welfare Act*, 1945, para. 1(a) (ii).
[3] *Hansard*, February 7, 1945, col. 2098.

Ten-year plans for development and welfare were requested in 1945 from the local colonial administrations by the Colonial Office with the stated purpose of enabling an apportionment of the Colonial Development and Welfare Fund by the central administration among the various territories.

Such plans were slow in coming forward due both to the continuing shortage of administrative personnel and to the general post-war shortages and uncertainties, and little had been done by the time of the sudden and deep financial crisis of 1947, which led to the revision of British economic policy at home and at the same time helped to speed up the shift of emphasis in colonial development policies from welfare to economic soundness. It had by then become an accepted tenet in London and it became one also, though somewhat more slowly, for the local officials dealing with planning and development problems in the various territories concerned that welfare and social development have to be paid for chiefly out of the resources of each territory and that therefore an increase in productive resources must be the main purpose of development. As a result of all these shortages and second thoughts development plans of an acceptable type only began to come forward in greater numbers towards the end of the 'forties and the beginning of the 'fifties.

(B) CHANGES IN THE POLICIES OF THE COLONIAL
TERRITORIES

The Pre-1940 Experience. The business of priority allocation and of detailed plan-making ultimately devolves upon the local authorities. The first *general* instruction to the colonial territories from the British Colonial Office which used the term 'development plans' was contained in Mr MacDonald's circular telegram No. 19 of February 20, 1940, which requested (as he himself informed the House of Commons) that plans should be drawn up by each territory for the expenditure of that territory's possible allocation from the £5 million a year grant. These first 'plans' were thus in fact only annual programmes for the spending of Colonial Development and Welfare Fund allocations.

But long-range plans, some of them fairly ambitious, had been drawn up long before this date in certain of the British colonial territories and to some extent implemented. Guggisberg, as Governor of the Gold Coast, seems to have been not only the first in the British colonial empire but also among the first in the modern world to put forward in outline in 1919 an integrated ten-year development plan.

The Guggisberg plan made provision for surveys and research as well as for actual development work and included both the aspects which have come to be known since as the economic and the welfare or social services aspects of development. It would be difficult today in Ghana to mention any major project, whether still under discussion or already implemented, which had not been investigated, sometimes in a fair amount of detail, under the impulse of the 1919 plan.[1]

In 1930 the Nyasaland Protectorate put forward, as a result of a demand by the Treasury in connection with certain Protectorate debts, a four-year development programme for 1931–4.

'In his despatch dated the 15th July 1930, notifying the acceptance by the Lords Commissioners of the Treasury of the proposal that the standard revenue (hitherto fixed at £300,000) after excluding postal revenue for the purpose of calculating the sums payable by the Protectorate under the Trans-Zambesia Railway guarantee should be raised to £450,000, the Secretary of State explained that the Treasury desire to receive with the draft estimates for 1931 a statement for the period from 1931 to 1934 inclusive, showing in respect of each year what expenditure it is proposed to charge against the additional revenue which is expected to be available, without recourse to surplus balances. This four-year programme of development is to show in the first place: (1) the capital expenditure which it is proposed to incur in each of the years, and (2) the recurrent expenditure which is to be charged against additional revenue, such expenditure to include not only (3) the recurrent charges involved in detailed schemes of development, whether already submitted or still under consideration locally, but also (4) provision for any expansion of Departments over and above the normal. Prominence is to be given in this scheme to (5) measures for increasing production (including (6) the improvement of the physical condition of the natives by (7) better nutrition and (8) the prevention of disease) and for facilitating (9) the increasing employment of natives in suitable posts at present held by Europeans. The expenditure on existing services is to be carefully re-

[1] The ten-year development plan for the Belgian Congo (put forward in 1920 by M. Franck) was a more restricted affair, as it was dealing only with public works. It is interesting in this context to point out the predominant influence of engineers and of Public Works administrators in connection with planned development throughout the colonial territories. The influence of the École Polytechnique has been all-pervasive in France, and Guggisberg was an engineer who had been in charge of the Public Works Department in Nigeria, from which he joined the Royal Engineers in the First World War before being appointed Governor of the Gold Coast.

viewed with the object of (i) effecting all feasible economies and (ii) substituting, where desirable, expenditure on new services more urgently required to secure the proper development of the Territory. (10) Taxation is to be increased when, and to the fullest extent, practicable.'[1]

Practically all the main directives for the British post-war development programmes were already contained in the above-quoted introductory note.

Other territories also had at various times either made longer-term development plans, usually of a sectional nature, or had established some kind of semi-permanent development body such as Uganda's Development Committee of 1936. As was rather impatiently put in *A Revised Plan of Development and Welfare for Nigeria 1951–56*:[2] 'Development is nothing new to Nigeria, whose history is one of development, and the revised plan deals only with the coming five years in this long history.' The impending visit of the Royal West India Commission was an especially strong incentive for attempts at the preparation of local development plans in the Caribbean. Trinidad and Tobago, and St Vincent, thus started their planning career in 1938 with this visit in mind. Nevertheless it is only the 1940–50 decade which has brought in development planning as a normal feature of government policy throughout all the British colonial territories.

The West Indies Planning Experiments. Few colonial administrations were in fact able or willing to undertake development plans while the war was in progress. The main exception was the West Indies, where development plans were closely connected with the comparatively massive grants from the Colonial Development and Welfare Fund and where a special organization had been set up as a result of the recommendations of the Moyne Commission. This central planning organization was established in 1940 under Sir Frank Stockdale, who was given the title of Comptroller of Development and Welfare in the West Indies. It was a body of experts who carefully checked and discussed each individual scheme and later on each individual plan put forward by the many dependencies in the West Indies, and advised on the allocation of existing funds to the various units.

[1] Nyasaland Protectorate: *Development Programme, 1931 to 1934*, 65 pp.; no date of publication. Introductory note (p. 3) dated Zomba, September 13, 1930. N.B. The itemizing (1) to (10) has been introduced by the author.
[2] Lagos, 1951, 146 pp.; p. 4, para. 5.

The need for such a multitude of fragmentary schemes and plans was mainly political. The reasons were very clearly explained by Sir Arthur Grimble, at the time Governor of the Windward Islands, when addressing the Legislature of the Windward Islands from St Vincent in April 1946 on the subject of the proposed amalgamation of the Leeward Islands and the Windward Islands.

'The insurance policy of every unit will, as I see the case, be none other than its authorized, long-range Plan of Development and Welfare.

'If each Government were to pledge itself to a Master Plan of such range and self-reliance, approved by His Majesty's Government, no colony need fear that its entry into political and financial union would entail upon its population any sacrifice that might have been avoided by a policy of isolation. The Central Government must indeed (as I have already said in other words) always command the power to distribute with due regard for every claim the annual revenue which comes into its hands. But, having the Master Plan of every Member of the Union always before it, it would be able at any budget meeting to act with an accuracy otherwise unobtainable, as the guardian of distributive justice to all. Beyond that, it would be bound by each plan as by a Charter, to justify its stewardship both to the Representatives of the Community concerned and to His Majesty's Government.'[1]

This fear of being at a disadvantage in a future local or Caribbean Federation seems thus to have been an important reason for having separate plans even for the Turks and Caicos Islands whose 'only considerable industry is salt-raking. All the salt is exported by the Salt Industry Board, and before the war exports averaged 50,000 tons annually',[2] or for the Cayman Islands covering 92·81 square miles and with a population of 6,670, as estimated in 1947.

In the dispersed and broken-up community of the West Indies of the 1940s Sir Frank Stockdale's organization, in co-operation at a certain stage with the Anglo-American Caribbean Commission, thus succeeded in claiming £1·8 million of the total of £2·86 million granted for the whole Colonial Empire by the British Government from the Colonial Development and Welfare Fund between 1940 and 1945. 'In other words, we spent by means of the organized machinery

---

[1] Cf. pp. i and ii from a *Plan of Development for the Colony of St Vincent, Windward Islands, British West Indies*, 1947.
[2] Cf. *Development Plan*, 1947.

under Sir Frank Stockdale, with its staff properly supplied with experts, twice as much on the 2,600,000 people as we had spent in the same time on the 50 million people in our great African colonies.'[1] The capacity for spending money is not necessarily the best indication of efficiency, nor can it even be entirely supposed that the only reason for the grant of CD & W funds in such a disproportionate manner was simply due to the greater realism in the presentation of worthwhile projects by Sir Frank Stockdale's organization as compared to the rest of the colonial territories. The West Indies had just been through a period of great political turmoil and the Colonial Office has always been especialy sensitive to unrest and disturbances. Nevertheless the work done both by the Moyne Commission and by the Stockdale organization was pioneer work and led logically not only to the further developments in Colonial Office policy but also, through the redistribution of colonial civil servants, to the spread throughout the colonial territories of many of the views and methods developed in the Caribbean laboratory.

Though Sir Frank Stockdale's organization by providing the individual experts, the team-work and the drive succeeded fairly rapidly in investigating many of the social and economic problems in the various West Indian territories and in giving more skilled advice on individual schemes to each administration than would otherwise have been possible, Sir Frank seems fairly soon to have come to the conclusion that such *ad hoc* advice was not sufficient, but that more integrated, overall plans were needed. In his report on *Development and Welfare in the West Indies, 1943-44*[2] he stated under the heading (g) *Public Works Projects*:

'... Extraordinary works should be planned well ahead and put into force as the occasion of the employment situation demands. Trinidad has set up a committee to plan and determine priority of its major extraordinary public works, and Jamaica is also preparing its plans. Barbados has announced a provisional five-year programme of public works. Rural as well as urban needs should be balanced as far as possible in order that the attraction of country people to the urban area is avoided.'

Such plans, with the Stockdale organization taking a very active part, advising, discussing and sometimes even drafting the plans themselves,

[1] Mr Riley, *Hansard*, February 7, 1945, col. 2153.
[2] *Colonial No. 189*, p. 17.

slowly began to come forward. Sir Frank Stockdale's translation to the Colonial Office in 1945 seems to have been made with the intention of making his experience gained in the Caribbean laboratory and his drive available to the local planners in the other colonial territories, and there is no doubt that that is how the House of Commons saw it. Some of the Members may have read even more into the appointment. Thus Mr de Rothschild (Liberal) thought Sir Frank's appointment indicated that there would be some kind of a master plan within which schemes would be scrutinized at the centre not only in the light of their value to each individual colony but of their value to the Empire as a whole.[1] Proposals were even put forward that Sir Frank should be given a fully fledged separate organization within the Colonial Office to deal with the local development schemes provided for under the 1945 Act. Such, of course, was not the intention of the Government.

The Beginning of Generalized Territorial Government Planning. It is difficult to say how seriously the central demand for a plan was at first taken locally. No colonial civil servant will of course say aloud that the Colonial Office does not know what it is doing on a matter of general policy, but it is difficult not to feel from reading between the lines of the first plans drafted in some of the colonies, or of the reasons given for not drafting them, that a certain amount of cynicism must have been present. It is also difficult not to sympathize, for example, with the administrator who, faced with a request for a ten-year plan, wrote that 'the chief obstacles in the way of formulating and carrying out a balanced and ordered programme of development are the lack of basic information, the lack of staff and the lack of money'.[2] There was, of course, also the other extreme, of visionary enthusiasm, such as is exemplified in some of the 'master plans' or 'long-term plans' established for certain, especially among the smaller, colonies such as British Honduras which, taking the Secretary of State's request for 'comprehensive plans'[3] very literally, tried to cover all desirable developments of which a vivid imagination could conceive. Though no generalization can be drawn, it seems that there may have been a tendency for the territories where the administration felt a greater need for outside financial and expert assistance to take development planning more seriously than the territories where the budgetary situation seemed less urgent, or the prospects less gloomy.

[1] Cf. *Hansard*, February 7, 1945, col. 2117.
[2] Cf. *Memorandum on Development in Sarawak*, 1947, p. 2.
[3] *Cmd 6713*.

On the whole, in these initial stages the procedure seems in quite a few territories to have tended at first towards a dilemma.

Either planning was not taken very seriously. In that case the planning committee and the drafting of the plan itself were left to relatively minor members of the administration or, if senior members were appointed to a committee, the plan was treated rather cavalierly, with the result in both cases that the plan tended to be forgotten as soon as it had been completed and forwarded to the Secretary of State. If the need was felt of reporting at regular intervals on the 'progress' of the plan (over and above the CD & W schemes, where yearly reports were compulsory) such reports were also usually entrusted to some fairly minor official. The results of such 'planning' was that the individual departments continued their own activities as before.

Or else planning was taken seriously. In that case a committee was appointed to which much significance was attached by the departments, whether it was a head of departments committee or a two- or three-man committee under the Chief Secretary or the Colonial Secretary (according to local nomenclature); each of the heads of the departments then tended to fight vigorously for the interests of his own department either to preserve the status quo or to take an at least equal share in any additional resources forthcoming under the plan. The result, as in the first case, tended to be that the relative positions of the various departments were again not appreciably affected by the introduction of these first plans.

Wherever there have been under such conditions variations in the allocations as between departments the reason can usually be traced to three main local factors: (i) shortages of men and materials which might affect some departments more than others; (ii) emergencies, especially of a political character, but sometimes also connected with unforeseen and unplanned changes in agricultural or mineral production or their world market prices; and (iii) the introduction in positions of authority of persons from outside the administration due to political developments which have led to the creation of 'unofficial', i.e. political as opposed to civil service, executives. All of these would no doubt have exercised similar influences if there had been no planning bodies at that stage.

A more specifically 'planning' influence leading to changes in allocations between sectors or departments has been connected with the overall directives coming from London. The metropolitan government's general approach to development expenditure seems to have varied (or at least to have given that impression to the territorial authorities) from a pre-1940 emphasis on the productive sector, to a greater emphasis on welfare until about 1946–7, and back to the productive sector since. In addition, differences in basic approach to the problems, and especially to the aims of planning, seem to have arisen from time to time between the metropolitan and certain of the territorial governments. These differences, which will be touched upon in the more detailed analysis of territorial plans undertaken further on, have normally resulted in the redrafting of the plans in accordance with Colonial Office suggestions.

Besides the West Indies, territories where Sir Frank Stockdale and later on Professor C. Y. Shepherd, together with their experts, were available for advice to each of the administrations, a small number of other territories also sought outside advice in the early stages of their respective planning attempts. *A Development Plan for Uganda* was drawn up by Mr E. B. Worthington and published in December 1946 in Entebbe. In Cyprus Professor Sir Patrick Abercrombie drew up a *Preliminary Planning Report*, published in July 1947. The *Report of the British Guiana and British Honduras Settlement Commission*, also known as the Evans Commission Report, made a number of development proposals for the two territories (*Cmd 7533*, September 1948). *A General Survey of the Somaliland Protectorate, 1944–50* (CD & W scheme D.484), which was undertaken by Mr John A. Hunt and published in 1951, could be looked upon as the basis for a development plan. Other territories entrusted the drafting of their plan to a specially detached 'expert' member of their own administrations. The British Guiana Ten Year Development Plan, 1947, was thus drawn up by a main development committee whose chairman was Mr Spencer, economic adviser to the Government of British Guiana, and in 1949 Mr H. Childs submitted, at the Governor's request, a report entitled *A Plan of Economic Development for Sierra Leone*.

The more recent International Bank of Reconstruction and Development surveys of Jamaica in 1952, of British Guiana in 1952–3, published in 1953, and of Nigeria in 1954, published in 1955, tend to fall within the later planning developments and are based on a fair amount of previous work.

THE FRENCH EXPERIENCE

The movement of British administrative opinion towards a policy of development planning in the colonial territories has been by no means an isolated event. Similar policies have been adopted, though not necessarily simultaneously, by most of the other colonial powers. In France colonial development policy has grown to be both more active and more integrated than in Britain. Originally the French approach seems to have been more strategic than economic, and to have reflected the predominance in official circles of the engineering, centralist conception of the Ecole Polytechnique. This led among other things to the insistence on the creation of main axes of communication without giving too much consideration to their immediate or even longer-term economic justification.

The French Imperial Conference of 1934–5. The many, private or official, proposals for development policies for the French colonial empire discussed before or during the First World War culminated in the carefully reasoned out and integrated system of projects put forward by Albert Sarraut in the French Parliament in 1921. But a full consideration by the government of the day of the whole problem of colonial development policies had to await the example of the United Kingdom Colonial Development Act of 1929. That Act, coupled with the French (and world) industrial crisis and with the public works experiments devised by the Blum Government to counter it, fostered the creation of a current of opinion centring round the idea, by no means new in French economic and political circles, of an 'Imperial Economy'. This culminated in the organization by the French Government in 1934–5 of an Imperial Economic Conference which included a broadly representative cross-section of both private and public interests and which proceeded to make detailed recommendations for the attainment of what might be loosely called an integrated autarchic imperial economy.[1] The immediate administrative result of the conference was the replacement of the annual North African Conference set up in 1923 by a North Africa High Commission set up on February 25, 1935. The High Commission had the advantage of a permanent office and secretary.

The conference decided that a Colonial Development Fund on the lines of the British Act of 1929 (as interpreted in France) should be set up with original grants by Parliament. The expenditures envisaged were of 15 billion francs over a period of fifteen years, of which 5 billion were to be allocated to the various territories over the first seven years and 6·2 billion over the following eight. The remaining 3·8 billion were to be used for undertakings of an imperial nature

[1] Cf. *Rapports généraux et conclusions d'Ensemble*, 1935, as summarized in *Le Monde Colonial*, Paris, May 1935.

which could not be allocated to specific territories or whose purpose was not necessarily economic and whose financing had therefore to be treated along different lines. The Trans-Sahara Railway seems to have been the main project of this kind envisaged at the time though it was left to the Pétain Government with the active encouragement of the German Government to make the most determined, though unsuccessful, efforts to put the project into effect.

The plan was fairly vague even for the first period of seven years; it was based on the idea of complementary economies according to which the Colonial Empire would expand its production of the raw materials needed by France, such as cotton and edible oils, by the investment of French funds into large-scale cultivation projects and by improvements in communications which would allow the draining of productive areas. The development fund was envisaged as a revolving fund in the optimistic belief that development schemes might fairly quickly be made sufficiently profitable to repay the original investments.

The purpose behind the decisions of the French Imperial Economic Conference of 1935 were thus appraised in 1937 by Melvyn M. Knight, Professor of Economics at the University of California:

'... with some exceptions, the scheme must be interpreted as a gesture to simulate unity and keep up morale. To get cotton and oil for France—in a world economy already suffocating in cotton and drowning in edible oils—five hundred million francs were earmarked for putting about a million acres of the Niger under cultivation. The cotton raised by irrigation far from existing transport facilities could not be cheap and the peanut oil supply was already sufficient and expensive. To call such schemes complementary economy is to employ a more or less deodorized synonym for autarchy.'[1]

In actual fact it is only now that the Niger Bend scheme, to which Professor Knight referred, is making some headway; the main activities of the French Government after the Imperial Conference and until the outbreak of the war concerned the improvement of communications, the 'opening-up' stage.

Post-war Plans. France was in no position to pass through the acts of faith of the Britain of 1940 and 1945. It could therefore start its post-war development plans in the somewhat more realistic mood of

[1] *Morocco as a French Economic Venture. A Study of Open-door Imperialism.*

1946–7. The purposes of the first comprehensive post-war (ten-year) French development plan[1] were polyvalent:
(1) The plan for the colonial territories was part of the plan for the whole of the French Union including France herself, and was thus further emphasizing the political union consecrated in the constitution. (2) The main problem to be tackled was the need for the integration of the native populations into the modern way of life. (3) A combined social and economic development was intended on the basis of large-scale contributions by France, especially in the form of investments which would lead to increased local production.

The purposes thus stated were wide enough, comprehensive enough and vague enough to remain constant since then, though serious doubts were to be raised and major changes of policy to take place concerning the best ways of implementing them.

THE BELGIAN EXPERIENCE

The first development plan for the Belgian Congo was outlined by King Leopold II in 1906. It concerned railways and mining. In 1920 an extensive programme of public works was put before the Belgian Parliament by M. Franck, and seems to have been carried out over a period of years.[2] The rapid expansion of the economy of the Belgian Congo during the Second World War, due chiefly to the Allied needs for its raw materials, especially its metals, greatly increased the importance of the territory for Belgium. In 1948–9 a specialist mission, which included both administrators and economists, was sent out by the Belgian Government and prepared, with the help of the local administration, a ten-year development plan. The aims of the development plan seem to have been mainly to enable the administration to overcome the difficulties of taking a long-term view while subject to a system of annual budgets, and to facilitate inter-departmental discussions on the best methods of co-operation for the purposes of a balanced development of the economic and social spheres in the Congo.[3] It is difficult to say whether the absence both of a visionary welfare approach, like that of the British Governments of 1940 and 1945, and of the bold undertakings of large-scale investments by the metropolitan government, as in the

[1] *Premier rapport de la commission de modernization des territoires d'outre-mer*, also known as the *Plan Pleven*, January 1948. Cf. especially pp. 9, 11 and 12.
[2] No detailed documents concerning the original Franck plan seem to have survived.
[3] *Plan décennal pour le développement économique et social du Congo Belge*, 1949, p. xii.

capital development plans of the French Union of 1947, were due to a more practical approach by the Belgian Government to the problems in hand or simply to the late date at which it was finally decided to embark on a plan, the Belgians having thus in a way benefited from the British and French experience and having lived their moments of enthusiasm by proxy.

THE NETHERLANDS EXPERIENCE

The Netherlands, deprived by the creation of Indonesia of most of their East Indies possessions which formed the bulk of their colonial empire, concentrated their post-war development efforts on Surinam (Dutch Guiana) and to a lesser extent on the Netherlands Antilles and Dutch New Guinea. Only in the case of Surinam has there been an attempt to draw up a development plan as now understood in the British, French and Belgian territories, neither the Antilles nor Dutch New Guinea lending themselves easily to such an exercise.

The States General (Netherlands Parliament) authorized[1] the Netherlands Government in 1947 to set up a Prosperity Fund under which they were to place at the disposal of Surinam N.Fl. 8 million a year for five years, or a total of N.Fl. 40 million. It was agreed that the Fund was insufficient to put Surinam on a sound economic basis, but its main purpose was to act as a stop-gap to enable a proper study to be made of the country's needs in preparation for a long-term development plan.

A Co-ordination Committee, financed through the Prosperity Fund, was set up in 1950, to include a Research Organization in The Hague and an Administrative Organization in Surinam itself, in Paramaribo. To make its position more official, the committee was transformed at the end of the year into a Planning Bureau, and on July 30, 1951, it finally became known as the Stichting Planbureau Suriname, an official organ of the Surinam Government.[2]

The preliminary studies undertaken in Surinam and centralized by the Stichting Planbureau were reviewed by a mission organized at the request of the Netherlands and Surinam Governments by the International Bank for Reconstruction and Development in September 1951. This mission's proposals were published in 1952. Political changes had been taking place meanwhile, resulting in the

---

[1] Surinam Planbureau: *Surinam's Development Possibilities*. Preliminary Report, 1951, Part 1, p. 4.
[2] Cf. *Samenvattend Eindverslag van het Welvaartsfonds Suriname*, 1955, pp. 266 ff.

setting up on December 29, 1954, of a tri-partite kingdom, with full internal sovereignty for the governments of Surinam and of the Antilles, with safeguards concerning foreign policy, and with participation in decisions of common interest by the representatives at The Hague of the 'Dominion' governments. In conjunction with the increased knowledge of the development problems of Surinam gained from the first development projects (undertaken outside the plan) this led to the need for a further redrafting of the ten-year development plan. The original plan, which had been placed before Parliament by the Surinam Government in August 1952 and which was still being discussed in 1954, was therefore revised by the Planbureau and was finally accepted by the Surinam Parliament on October 9, 1954. January 1, 1955, was set as its starting date, but it was to include a certain number of projects already under way.[1]

THE GENERAL ACCEPTANCE OF PLANNING

It may be said that by 1950 the colonial powers mentioned in this study as well as their colonial territories were all agreed on the need for development programmes spread over a number of years, and their administrations had been or were being geared to draw up and implement such programmes. Certain basic differences remained. Some were of scale: Surinam is thus only a fraction of the French and British territories. Some were of homogeneity: the Belgian Congo and Ruanda-Urundi form a territorially unitary block; the French Union is made up of many separate units, each of which puts up its own development proposals which are then (or have been until recently) dovetailed by a number of central organizations into an overall programme so that the whole Union moves in step; finally, in the British colonial empire each territory has worked entirely separately from all the others; any synchronization of plans has been almost entirely coincidental; planning organizations and detailed approaches to the problems in hand have varied right through; and only certain very general impulses have been sent out from the centre, usually in connection with the use of the funds allocated as grants or loans to the individual territories by the United Kingdom.

[1] Cf. *Surinam in the Making*, 1955, pp. 5 ff; *Samenvattend Eindverslag van het Welvaartsfonds Suriname*, 1955; Stichting Planbureau Suriname: *Tienjarenplan foor Suriname*, 1955, p. 1.

PART IV

PLANNING MACHINERIES

CHAPTER 6

The Metropolitan Governments' Planning Machineries

ADMINISTRATIVELY speaking, colonial planning may roughly be divided into planning by the metropolitan governments and planning within each of the colonial territories. In the case of the colonial powers touched upon in this study both aspects of planning are apparent, but their relative importance and their inter-relationships have varied considerably from case to case. For reasons of convenience the metropolitan aspects of planning will be discussed first and the territorial aspects, which, especially in the case of the British territories, tend to be more complex, afterwards and their inter-relationships will be pointed out *pari passu*.

BRITAIN

In Britain the views on the best machinery for metropolitan government planning have fluctuated to some extent but three main points seem to have tended to win the day.

The first is that any central, overall or specialized planning committee (or committees) should be a 'purely advisory committee. The responsibility rests with the Secretary of State and with him alone. . . .'[1]

The second is that it is on the whole better not to have overall planning in the sense of one integrated plan for the whole of the colonial empire. The plans should be drafted in each colony separately by the local, administrative or other, authorities responsible, on the basis at most of a small number of guiding lines from the centre. The detailed steps in this planning procedure were thus summarized by Mr MacDonald in 1940:

'. . . Already we have communicated to the various colonial governments, as a first step, a request that they should prepare

[1] Mr MacDonald: *Hansard*, May 21, 1940, col. 121.

their plans of development. We have given to each of them some preliminary and tentative indication of the sort of sum out of the total of £5,000,000 which they might expect to get for expenditure in their own territories. At this moment the governments in the colonies, with that general idea of the kind of expenditure upon which they may be able to count, are drawing up their plans under the various heads. . . . We are now awaiting the submission of plans from the local governments drawn up with their local experience and knowledge. . . . It may be our view from our knowledge of affairs in other colonies that in the case of Colony "A" too little importance is being attached to something like technical education. . . . The whole of the plan will be passed and will proceed, but . . . subsequently communications will be sent to the colonial government concerned raising this particular question and asking them to consider it, and let us have their views on it, with regard to plans of development for the following year.'[1]

Five years later Colonel Stanley re-emphasized and illustrated the reasons for this de-centralizing approach to planning:

'I have made it plain that there must be no question of detailed planning done in this country. It is not the idea of the administration of the Act to impose on the colonies a new heaven prefabricated in Whitehall. In the first place you cannot do that sort of planning efficiently here in this country. We cannot sit round the table here, and say if they are going to have fifteen new schools in Jamaica, what are the exact sites on which to put them. Apart from any question of doing it officially, it is wrong to try to do so because you have to allow the maximum opportunity for the people of the territory themselves to be associated with this planning, since it is their future that is being planned. It is their life that is affected and therefore it is they who must have the greater say.'[2]

The third is that, though expert bodies attached to the Colonial Office have a very important rôle to play in the later stages of the development of the individual plans, it might be preferable to have separate expert bodies to one single overall advisory council. This has been a more controversial issue, with a fair amount of compromise on both sides.

The allocations under the 1929 Colonial Development Act had thus

[1] *Hansard*, May 21, 1940, cols. 119–20.
[2] Ibid., February 7, 1945, col. 2105.

been made on the recommendation of a central advisory committee, but already in the debate on the 1929 Bill the possibility of 'duplicate bodies for undertaking different sorts of work' had been put forward as a preferable alternative to the single advisory committee.[1] The arguments in favour of this proposal were concerned with the difference in return to investments: some investments lead to immediate and obvious returns, whereas others, such as research or technical education, are long-term investments where returns are difficult to calculate in monetary terms. Hence different types of bodies which would be able to look at money allocations from different points of view—'advice as to the grant for research must be given on quite different grounds from advice as to a guarantee for an economic undertaking'[2]—were considered advisable.

Lord Hailey, in connection with the African Survey, which he started in the late 'thirties at the request of the Colonial Office, had put forward his own reasons for the need for some central advisory body to concentrate on problems of research. Mr MacDonald in his 1940 proposals endorsed Lord Hailey's views and stated the Government's intention to set up two separate advisory committees, a Colonial Development and Welfare Advisory Committee under the chairmanship of Lord Moyne, and a Colonial Research Committee under the chairmanship of Lord Hailey.[3]

The proposed sphere of activity of the Colonial Research Committee seemed sufficiently clear not to need further elucidation, but Mr MacDonald was at some pains to outline the tasks to be allotted to the Colonial Development and Welfare Advisory Committee. The committee was to scrutinize individual plans to see if a proper balance between the various major items of expenditure had been struck; and possibly more important, it would perform 'another extremely useful function': it would act as a co-ordinating and advisory body to the authorities both in London and in the colonies. In London, by considering the claims of each colony with due regard to those of the others, it could give the necessary advice to the Secretary of State for the Colonies on how the £5 million should be shared out each year. In the colonies, by having an overall picture of the problems throughout the Empire it could more easily see when individual patterns of development tended to get out of balance by undue emphasis in one or the other direction.[4]

[1] Sir Hilton Young, *Hansard*, July 12, 1929, col. 1282.
[2] Cf. *op. cit.*
[3] Cf. Second Reading of the Colonial Development and Welfare Bill, *Hansard*, May 21, 1940.
[4] Cf. Mr MacDonald: *Hansard*, May 21, 1940, col. 120.

The rapid deterioration in the war situation forced the Government to reconsider their proposals, as it was felt that nobody could really be spared at the time from their much more urgent duties elsewhere to serve on these committees, and Mr Hall was forced to inform the House of Commons[1] that the setting up of these two committees had to be indefinitely deferred. Nevertheless, the decision to have two separate committees had not been abandoned and on April 28, 1942, it was possible to announce in Parliament that the Colonial Research Committee had now been set up as originally foreseen under the chairmanship of Lord Hailey. A modified Colonial Development and Welfare Advisory Committee was also set up internally in the Colonial Office to include only officials and was put at first under the chairmanship of the Marquess of Dufferin and Ava, and, on the transfer of the marquess to other duties, under that of Mr Harold Macmillan.

The Government's decision in 1945 to bring before Parliament a new Colonial Development and Welfare Act led to a new appraisal of the problem of a central advisory committee. The need for a separate committee to deal with research schemes had by now been generally accepted, but the Colonial Secretary of State had obviously come to have doubts concerning the usefulness of a single Colonial Development and Welfare Advisory Committee. In answer to a proposal put forward by Major Henderson for the creation of a central advisory committee which would discuss major issues arising under the new Act, Colonel Stanley, the Colonial Secretary of State, put forward the opposite view to that advanced in 1940 by Mr MacDonald. He upheld a system of separate advisory committees for each of the various technical subjects by pointing out that it would be impossible to find one single small group of people who could give specialist advice on programmes including such varied matters as 'health, agriculture, veterinary services and fishing and so on'. He therefore advocated a 'functional provision of advice' by individual experts and technicians (of which he stated the Colonial Office had many) rather than an overall committee if the best advice possible on such difficult subjects was wanted.[2]

The only concession made by him to the need for some overall guidance and advice was the appointment, already referred to, of a person experienced in problems of colonial development—Sir Frank Stockdale—as Adviser on Development Planning.[3] That post was

[1] Cf. Third Reading of the CD & W Bill: *Hansard*, June 11, 1940.
[2] *Hansard*, February 7, 1945, cols. 2185–6.
[3] Colonel Stanley: *Hansard*, Oral Answers, January 24, 1945, col. 814.

created as part of the Colonial Office organization with the stated purpose of assisting the Secretary of State in the 'co-ordination' of the plans for social and economic development, and it seems to have lapsed with Sir Frank's death some two years later.

It is possible to wonder whether one of the objections to the kind of advisory committee put forward by Mr MacDonald and again suggested by Major Henderson may not have been a dislike by the Colonial Office of the inclusion of 'unofficial' members, which both the 'internal' committee of 1942 and the appointment of Sir Frank Stockdale neatly avoided, but which was obviously in the minds of the supporters of such an advisory committee.

With a Labour government in power this question was once more reconsidered by the new Secretary of State and a Colonial Economic and Development Council, with a mixed official and unofficial membership, was set up in September 1946, under Viscount Portal as its first chairman. The stated task of the council was to advise the Secretary of State for the Colonies on the framing and subsequent review of plans for economic and social development in the colonial empire and on questions of general economic and financial policy.

Fairly active at first while development plans were being forwarded from the colonies for review and discussion the council was left with less and less to do once the plans had been approved and had begun to be implemented. The Secretary of State therefore decided in 1951, with the Conservatives once more in power, to discontinue it. The work of advice henceforward devolved entirely upon the normal organization of the Colonial Office, coming to rely more and more, as Colonel Stanley had specified, on the individual expert opinion of the officials specializing in the various matters with which the Colonial Office had to deal.

The only overall aspects of colonial planning to which a growing importance has been attached throughout have been the collection and centralization, within the Colonial Office, of statistical information, the economic interpretation of such data, as well as the regular publication both in detail and in digest form of such information. The Colonial Office has thus been drifting away from even its restricted participation in the planning for development in the colonial territories towards the more aloof position of recording angel. This is in keeping both with the heterogeneous character of the British colonial empire, most unsuited to highly centralized systems of government, and with the British Government's policy of preparing the individual colonial territories for self-government by allotting to them rapidly increasing administrative, economic and political responsibilities.

This attitude is, of course, not the only one possible. It is interesting to contrast it with that adopted by other colonial powers.

FRANCE

The first 'plan for the modernization and equipment of the French overseas territories' was completed in November 1947 and published in January 1948, but it took into account development projects started since the end of the war. It followed the outline indicated by M. Gaston Monnerville in his report put before the National Constituent Assembly on behalf of the Commission of the Overseas Territories on April 5, 1946. The plan adopted the proposals made on March 7, 1946, to the National Constituent Assembly by M. Jacques Soustelle and a number of deputies for the creation of a fund for the economic and social equipment of the French Union; and the proposals made by M. Gaston Monnerville two days later for the establishment, financing and implementation of a plan for the organization, equipment and development of the overseas territories.

The Planning Commission was established as part of the wider organization, dealing with the whole of the French Union including metropolitan France, which is known as the 'Commissariat général au Plan' and which is an advisory committee to the Prime Minister. M. Pleven, a former minister for Overseas France and a financial expert, was given the task of chairing the commission and had a major part in the drafting of the report which came to be known as the Pleven Plan. There seems to be some disagreement on whether the desire for a wide participation by experts in the elaboration of a central plan for overseas France, or some lingering memories of the 1934–5 Imperial Economic Conference or, more simply, the accidental availability of M. Pleven, was the main reason for the establishment of that first post-war commission in a mixed form to include both officials and non-officials, but the precedent has by now been firmly established. The commission, few of whose members came from the colonies, was subdivided into sub-commissions: on agricultural production, forestry, mining, public works, town planning and social problems. The report gave general guiding lines on the main problems and on the methods recommended to cope with them. It also put forward very detailed estimates of the sums to be spent on individual projects throughout the territories during the following ten years, on the basis of two five-year periods, the first from 1946 to 1951 and the second from 1951 to 1956.

The two main financing agencies had already been established by the Act of April 30, 1946. The first was the Caisse Centrale de la France d'Outre-Mer (CCFOM) with an overall accounting and budgetary control over the second organization, the Fond d'Investissement et de Développement Economique et Social (FIDES) and with powers of advancing money to public as well as to private bodies and enterprises. CCFOM was also given a watching brief over the whole economic and monetary situation in the overseas territories, which made of it a permanent advisory body both to the central and to the local authorities. FIDES was established as the grant-making body for all development projects throughout the French territories on the basis at first of half or two-thirds participation in the total costs of the projects. This proportion has been steadily increasing, and has already reached 90 per cent, the remaining 10 per cent being usually drawn as a loan from CCFOM.

The actual establishment of annual budgets for the overseas territories has been incumbent in as far as the metropolitan contributions are concerned upon the Minister for Overseas Territories, who has his own advisory body made up of officials of his ministry (the Direction du Plan) and who acts in consultation with the administrations of the territories concerned.

The first five-year, 1946–51, period of the Pleven Plan was more realistically transformed for purposes of accountancy and planning discussions into a four-year, 1948–52, period which was itself prolonged into 1953 while the second four-year plan was being drafted. That plan was finally accepted to cover the period from 1954 to 1957 inclusive. For purposes of accountancy it has now been back-dated to 1953.

This second plan was a compromise plan, the chairman (this time an 'official', Governor Roland Pré) disagreeing with the commission, which was again constituted mainly of metropolitan—official and non-official—members but which was now able to base itself more solidly on the experience and results of a previous plan.

To avoid the delays caused by the rather tardy appointment by the Government of their second planning commission and by the procedural difficulties involved before the planning commission's recommendations could be accepted, the drafting of the third plan was taken in hand soon after the official start of the second plan. The Government undertook at the same time a complete reappraisal of the political and administrative framework within the territories coming under the Ministry for Overseas France. As a result of this reappraisal a new Act was passed on June 23, 1956, which introduced in each of the individual colonial territories universal suffrage, elected assemblies, and governments responsible to those assemblies. It is difficult to foresee as yet the effect of these changes on the existing system of development planning but there is little doubt that local views will have a much greater importance in the future. On the other hand, as almost the whole of the 'development' funds are at present derived from grants and loans made by the metropolitan government and will probably continue to be so derived for an indefinite period ahead, the various central planning organizations will continue to have an important word to say in the final allocations.

BELGIUM AND THE NETHERLANDS

Both the Belgian Congo (with Ruanda-Urundi) and Surinam are territorially compact colonies. The problem of centralization versus separate territorial plans does therefore not arise in similar terms. There is nevertheless still the problem of whether the planning should be done from the perspective of the mother-country or of the colony, or through some joint body.

The Belgians decided, as we have seen, on a specialist team from Brussels to investigate the position and to take into account the proposals of the administrative bodies in the Congo. There was also some consultation of certain of the business interests both in Belgium and in the Congo itself, but on the whole the tendency has been rather to avoid too close a contact with such interests. As the Congo Government has itself large interests in the Congo mining enterprises, no doubt part of the problems of such enterprises must have been taken into account through the views put forward by the government representatives on their boards.

The ten-year plan thus established in 1949 began to operate from 1950 and has been left entirely under the direction of the Government of the Belgian Congo, whose contacts with the Ministry of Colonies in Brussels tend to be those of partnership and of access to expert advice. As there is no elected decision-making body in the Belgian Congo, its administrative service is in fact also the Congo Government, and the Colonial Office acts as the link between that administration and the Belgian Cabinet and Parliament.

In the case of Surinam, where there was an elected Assembly and Cabinet, the Dutch Government has tended to act only as a source of funds, of planning initiative and of technical and expert advice, including the provision of a fairly large number of Dutch technicians from the former Dutch East Indies who are now available for direct employment by the Surinam authorities.

In conjunction with the setting up of the tri-partite kingdom, it was agreed in December 1954 by the Governments of the Netherlands and of Surinam that the Netherlands should set up a mission in Surinam which should advise on the practicability and advisability of each project. The mission was set up in 1955.

The actual drafting, supervision and implementation of the plan has been left to local bodies. On March 15, 1955, the Stichting Planbureau thus became the co-ordinating body for implementing the plan, work on which was undertaken by various departments. Since January 1, 1956, all projects within the plan come under a separate department, which is responsible also for all new project authorizations.[1]

[1] Cf. Stichting Planbureau Suriname: *Verslag 1954–6 Tienjarenplan Suriname* 1957, p. 1.

CHAPTER 7

The Territorial Governments' Planning Machineries I

A CASE STUDY

A DEVELOPMENT plan necessitates an approach to income and expenditure estimates different from that of the usual annual budgeting of a territorial government. Forecasting of both future resources and future needs *must* be made over a much longer period than the accustomed one. And the year-by-year changes of policy which, under an annual budgetary system, arise from or are reflected in fairly small variations in taxation or in expenditure *may* have to be replaced by a reappraisal of the situation as a whole and by a change of direction covering all aspects of government activity. While longer-term forecasting is to some extent a problem in techniques of budgeting and as such mainly a problem of an administrative character, a reappraisal of the situation as a whole, in which the question of 'priority' decisions looms largest, is most closely related to the devising of a new political programme such as would be put forward in a democratic country as an election platform by the contending parties. Any purely administrative arrangements made to draw up and implement a development plan will sooner or later have to face up to this need for combining the administrative and the political aspects of planning. This is especially difficult in the bureaucratic type of colonial governments with which we are dealing; and changes in some of these governments towards a more representative character *while* plans are being worked out make such a combination even more complicated.

Keeping in mind the existence of these twin aspects of a development plan, the administrative and the political, its organizational stages could be outlined as follows:

The *first* stage involves an investigation into the basic quantities concerned, on the income as well as on the expenditure side. This is normally a purely administrative problem.

In the *second* stage the plan itself has to be drawn up by deciding on the priorities to be allocated on the basis of the information collected. The main decisions in this second stage must have a political character.

In the *third* stage the planning decisions taken must be implemented. This is, like the first stage, an administrative job. These three stages cover, in theory at least, the whole of the plan. In fact such a plan tends to be only the first of a series.

A *fourth* stage, therefore, must be taken into account, namely that of the preparation for the next plan. This could be looked upon as a transitional, connecting stage linking up one plan with the next. It involves a review of the third stage, that of implementation, of the first plan concommitantly with the setting up of machinery to deal with the first and second stages as outlined above for the plan to follow.

And thus *ad infinitum*. With increasing experience and with changes in the economic, social and political backgrounds, the scope, the methods and the organizations related to planning will tend, of course, to vary from plan to plan.

A CASE STUDY: KENYA

There is no well-established practice on the best solution to the administrative problems involved in these planning stages, nor is it possible to find an example which could be considered typical. The experience of Kenya, stretching over a number of plans and covering many changes in its economic and political background, seems, though, to have covered a fair number of the problems to be encountered and of their possible solutions, and it will therefore be used to illustrate the working of the machinery of development planning and priority allocation, in the hope that the more detailed analysis of this machinery will then be a little easier to follow.

Approach to Development Planning. Under the 1940 CD & W Act a number of *individual* schemes were prepared and put forward for assistance from the CD & W Fund. In 1943 the Governor, Sir Henry Moore, drew attention to the need for a general plan for development.[1] Early in 1944, under the further impulse of Colonial Paper No. 3 on Development Planning, the Kenya Government considered that the time was ripe for the preparation in detail of such a general plan of development.

Collection of Basic Information. Accordingly, in a Secretariat Circular Letter (No. 4 of May 20, 1944) five-year departmental plans

[1] Cf. *Despatch No. 112* of August 6, 1943 and *Sessional Paper No. 51* of 1955. para. 15, p. 5.

were requested from all the chief departments of the Government, to be handed in before the end of July 1944; and similar provincial plans, framed with due regard for the plans prepared by the heads of departments, were to be forwarded before the end of December 1944.

Setting Up the Development Committee. In January 1945 a Development Committee was appointed for the purpose of preparing development plans for the colony, taking into account departmental and provincial plans prepared in response to the Circular Letter.[1]

Implementation of the Plan. On the basis of proposals put forward by the Government of Kenya and laid before the Legislative Council[2] a Development and Reconstruction Authority (DARA) was set up on August 1, 1945. The Development and Reconstruction Authority was going to be responsible to the Governor for the expenditure of all sums specifically allocated for development and reconstruction plans. It was recommended and agreed that, as an authority charged with such comprehensive duties would necessarily impinge upon what had hitherto been regarded as the special functions of individual government departments, its chairman should be the Chief Secretary and that he should assume for the time being the additional rôle of Member of the Executive Council (i.e. the equivalent of Minister) for Development and Reconstruction. In order to enable the Chief Secretary to devote himself primarily to the problems of development and reconstruction it was further proposed that the Deputy Chief Secretary should undertake those duties which would normally fall to the Chief Secretary.[3]

The decision to charge DARA with executive responsibility for the ten-year plan led to the colony's estimates being divided as from January 1, 1946, into two parts: the first devoted to ordinary government revenue and expenditure; and the second comprising the revenue and expenditure relating to development and reconstruction. In the same estimates a Development and Reconstruction Fund was established into which were to be paid all moneys earmarked for capital expenditure on development and reconstruction over a period of years. This was intended to ensure that DARA should be free as far as possible from uncertainty in regard to the amount of money available to undertake the programme of development and reconstruction to be assigned to it, 'an uncertainty rendered

[1] Cf. *Report of the Development Committee*, vol. 1, 1946, paras. 4, 5.
[2] *Sessional Paper No. 3*, June 25, 1945.
[3] Cf. DARA *Report*, 1947, chap. 1, paras. 1, 2.

inevitable by the normal system of colonial estimating for an annual balanced budget'. The Authority met formally at various times in the year, but much of the consultation of members was done informally by the circulation of papers and direct personal contact with the permanent staff. The Authority had also to make an annual report to the Governor in Council, to be laid upon the Table of the Legislative Council, upon the progress of all works and projects for which it was responsible, and the state of the fund at its disposal, and to give an outline of the ensuing year's work.[1]

Revision of the Plan. On July 2, 1948, the Governor in Council approved of the setting up of a Planning Committee consisting of the members of the Authority and of certain co-opted official and unofficial planning members as proposed in the Report of the first Development Committee (vol. i, para. 8) to revise the original development plan.[2]

The Planning Committee, which was established towards the end of 1948, immediately encountered two serious difficulties. In the first place, it soon became apparent that a great deal more than a mere revision of existing plans was required, as the plans were by then completely out of date.

In the second place, so many new projects were being pressed for by the public, 'all of them more or less urgent and eminently desirable', that to include them all in the revised plans would have necessitated funds greatly in excess of the amount of finance in sight. Hence the committee's task as outlined by the Governor in Council 'appeared to be a virtually impossible one'.

New Collection of Data. As a result of these two serious difficulties the committee suspended its operations whilst a financial review was carried out to ascertain the total which could be made available to finance development over the balance of the period. The members of the Planning Committee having expressed their strong views on the need for a system of continuous planning to keep in step with the rapid changes in 'a young and growing colony like Kenya', the Government decided to consider a re-organization of the planning side of development with a view to the establishment of a permanent or Standing Planning Committee.[3] As a result of ensuing discussions the Governor directed in March 1950 that the Planning Committee

[1] *Government Notice No. 674*, published on August 2, 1945. Point 10.
[2] Cf. *Report of the Planning Committee*, 1951, Introduction.
[3] Cf. *Annual Report of DARA for 1949*, 1950, p. 4.

should be reconstituted as a Standing Planning Committee, with the same terms of reference as the Planning Committee it was superseding.[1]

On January 1, 1951, a separate bank account was opened for the Development and Reconstruction Authority to which the cash and investments belonging to the Development and Reconstruction Fund were transferred. This was done because it had become apparent in 1950 that the form in which the DARA estimates and financial statement were presented led to some confusion.[2]

Appointment of New Planning Committee and Abolition of Standing Planning Committee and of DARA. In its Report the Planning Committee had carefully defined the respective spheres of the proposed permanent Planning Committee and of DARA. The permanent Planning Committee was to keep the situation under review and, as priorities altered, to re-define the targets from time to time as and when required. DARA was to continue to have responsibility for assigning priority of execution 'as between works and projects approved'.[3]

But the committee had not foreseen some of the political problems involved. The main difficulty was that the arrangements did not tie in very neatly with the over-all responsibility of the Government for policy, subject to the usual powers of the Legislative Council. For example, it was felt that schemes which might be regarded by the Government as of the highest importance from a policy point of view could be 'modified, varied or cut out altogether' by the Standing Planning Committee guided by development criteria.

The particular phase in development planning for which the Standing Planning Committee had been specifically appointed could be interpreted to have come to an end with the completion of the 'master plan' for the period 1951–5. The Governor in Council felt therefore doubly justified in dissolving, in May, 1952, the existing Standing Planning Committee and in replacing it by a sub-committee of the Executive Council, consisting of the Chief Secretary, the Financial Secretary, the Chief Native Commissioner, the Deputy Chief Secretary and the four unofficial members. Planning became then a function of the Executive Council. The plans proposed by the Executive Council, where they varied from those put forward in the Standing Planning Committee's Report, were to be considered by

[1] Cf. *Report of the Planning Committee*, 1951, p. 1.
[2] *Annual Report of DARA for 1950*, p. 7.
[3] Cf. *Report of the Planning Committee,* 1951, para. 34.

the Legislative Council in connection with that year's debate—the last—of the Annual Estimates of DARA.

The reorganization involved also certain of the functions performed until then by DARA. DARA itself was dissolved, as its main duty, of determining priorities between works and projects approved, could no longer be carried out, all its funds having been already fully committed for the ten-year period. The financial control for development expenditure now devolved upon the Treasury, and individual members, in addition to being spending agents for funds voted by the Legislative Council, became also spending authorities. The Executive Planning Sub-Committee invited the members (i.e. the equivalent of ministers in charge of departments) to state what changes and revisions they wanted to suggest for the development plan, and on October 9, 1952, it met to consider such proposals, some of which it decided to recommend to the Legislative Council.

New Plan. However, with the prolongation of the emergency due to the Mau Mau rising and the rapidly changing circumstances facing the colony the Government decided in April 1953 that a completely revised development programme for the three-and-a-half-year period January 1, 1954, to June 30, 1957, should be drawn up.[1]

New Development Committee, and Further Reorganization of the Implementation Stage. In 1954 the Secretary of State for the Colonies visited Kenya and as a result of his visit a Council of Ministers was appointed by additional (royal) instructions dated April 13, 1954. The council, appointed with effect from April 20, 1954, consisted of six unofficial and two nominated members. The Secretary of State also announced his intention to establish under the chairmanship of the Minister for Finance and Development, a Development Committee which was going to be responsible to the Council of Ministers for keeping the development and building programmes under review and for making recommendations on the question of priorities. In addition, the Development Committee was also to provide any co-ordination necessary to ensure the speedy implementation of the plan. Financial control remained the responsibility of the Treasury and works execution devolved upon the Ministry of Works.[2]

With the abolition of DARA the whole system of a double budget

[1] Cf. *Sessional Paper No. 51* of 1955, paras. 21–5.
[2] Cf. *Cmd Paper 9103, Kenya; Proposals for the Reconstruction of the Government.* HMSO, 1954; and *Kenya; Sessional Paper No. 51*, 1955, para. 27.

also began to seem anomalous, as the 'mere existence of a development programme' did not seem to justify an arrangement to which the Government felt there were certain objections both fiscal and especially from the point of view of the legislative control of expenditure. As, in addition, it did not prove easy to separate the two budgets along what seemed to be to the Government the obvious lines of a capital budget and a recurrent expenditure budget, the Government decided to consider the possibility of the adoption of a single budget system 'in accordance with United Kingdom practice', with expenditure financed from money loans being shown below-the-line.[1]

CONCLUSIONS

In the above examples from Kenya, the four stages may thus be easily and repeatedly followed, though under changing circumstances.

(i) The first collection of basic quantities was undertaken on a departmental and provincial basis by the existing administrative organs, each for its own sphere, and centralized in the Secretariat.

(ii) An *ad hoc* committee, partly of officials and partly of unofficials, was then given the political task of allocating priorities on the basis of these data.

(iii) The implementation of the plan was then entrusted to the control of a specially-set-up Development and Reconstruction Authority, itself closely integrated through its guiding personnel into the administrative machine.

(iv) The need for a revision of the plan having made itself felt, a new Planning Committee was set up, similarly constituted as the first one, to make new decisions and priorities on the basis of information forthcoming from the administration, thus starting a new cycle, etc.

This fourfold pattern will, of course, be found throughout the territories involved in planning exercises. But the details at each stage, and often the transition between stages, can be quite different, both as between territories and, as we have seen from the above example, even as between successive plans within the same territory, especially when the political background changes. An attempt will therefore be made to analyse the whole process of planning, stage by stage, for the four main stages outlined above, and to indicate and exemplify the variations on each theme as between some of the territories involved.

[1] Cf. *Kenya; Sessional Paper No. 51,* 1955, para. 98.

CHAPTER 8

The Territorial Governments' Planning Machineries II

THE COLLECTION OF DATA

(A) RELATING TO EXPENDITURE

The 'Departmental' Approach. In our basic example of Kenya the data relating to expenditure was, as we saw, collected in accordance with the arbitrary divisions of central government departments, and in a subsidiary fashion from the provincial administrations which were instructed to take into account the previously drawn up departmental estimates. In the British territories this seems to have been the most usual approach to the problem of collecting data concerning estimated expenditure, though, of course, there were many variations of detail as between territories.

Thus in Uganda the Development and Welfare Committee published *An Outline of Post-War Development Proposals as submitted to the Development and Welfare Committee for Consideration*, in which it stated that it felt it necessary to stress that the plan (which was its first post-war plan) was not in the strict sense a co-ordinated protectorate plan. It was in the main an aggregation of departmental proposals which the Secretary summarized, and which he supplemented by certain chapters, e.g. on social services, on demobilization, and on other subjects which were not at the time the concern of any particular department.[1]

In Northern Rhodesia the sub-committee of the Native Development Board asked the heads of the social and economic services departments to draw up detailed plans and estimates for their own departments over a ten-year period. These were completed in April 1945. The plan for each department was intended to indicate the minimum expansion necessary for each department over ten years, without including any 'luxury' services of any kind.[2]

In Malaya the Economic Development Committee recommended that a ten-year development programme should be drawn up, divided,

---

[1] Cf. Uganda Protectorate: *Joint Report of the Standing Finance Committee and the Development and Welfare Committee on Post-War Development*, para. 10. No date of publication.
[2] Cf. *Ten Year Development Plan for Northern Rhodesia*, 1948, para. 5.

according to Colonial Office instructions, into two five-year periods. Heads of departments in the Malayan Union Government were as a result asked to submit ten-year development programmes, in outline, for their departments, giving approximate estimates of costs. These departmental programmes were to be co-ordinated into a plan for a ten-year development programme on the basis of the funds estimated to be available. The plan was to include, in addition to estimated capital expenditure, also all the important increases in the recurrent expenditure of the departments dealing with Public Health, Agriculture and other developmental services.[1]

In Cyprus the Planning Committee looked on the task of drawing up a comprehensive scheme of development covering all branches of the administration as falling into two reasonably well-defined parts. The first part comprised the departmental plans most nearly concerned with general development, namely the Agricultural, Irrigation, Forests, Medical and Education Departments plans. The second part related to more miscellaneous activities such as harbours, communications, municipal schemes, village improvements, housing, archaeology (with special reference to the encouragement of tourism), and others.[2]

In Zanzibar detailed departmental programmes with estimates of costs were prepared with a view to their embodiment in a comprehensive development plan. For the purpose of determining the implications of a ten-year plan (i.e. 1946–55) as laid down by the Secretary of State, the departments were informed that actual expenditure incurred during 1944 was to be accepted as the norm and that any new services or expansions of existing services introduced or contemplated after January 1, 1945, were to be treated as development services.[3]

In Nigeria the heads of the departments principally concerned with development programmes were requested to submit a scheme of expansion of services and facilities based upon departmental policies and upon the recommendations which had been made by the Provincial Development Committees. In some cases departments dealing with basic physical developments such as roads and water supplies were in a position to submit a complete plan at relatively short notice either because policies were already fairly well established or because it was not difficult to work out a scheme of development

---

[1] Cf. *Progress Report of the Development of the Federation of Malaya 1950–2*, 1953, p. 1.
[2] Cf. *A Ten Year Programme of Development for Cyprus*, 1946.
[3] *Programme of Social and Economic Development in the Zanzibar Protectorate for the Ten Year Period 1946–55*, 1946, para. 3.

based arithmetically upon population. Other departments were able to prepare approximate schemes, the details of which required further consideration both locally and in the Colonial Office. Even in cases in which a detailed development plan could not be formulated at short notice rough estimates of the costs of developments were nevertheless provided by the departments concerned. On completion, these departmental schemes were to be integrated into one overall 'rough outline plan' which was then to be broken down into a series of regional, provincial and village projects.[1]

In the Gold Coast the heads of departments were invited to prepare ten-year plans on an individual basis and without regard to the amount of funds which were eventually to be available for distribution. Meanwhile a financial survey was undertaken and when it became obvious that the majority of the plans would require to be modified in the light of this survey, the modification was still conceived of as on a 'departmental basis'.[2]

In the Gambia the preparation of a detailed ten-year programme was begun on the lines laid down in Colonial No. 3 on *Development and Welfare*. The announcement of the funds available to the Gambia in the Secretary of State's Circular Despatch of November 12, 1945, involved considerable reductions in the programme and it was proposed that a grant for general development should be divided between the Medical, Education, Agriculture and Veterinary Departments. The departments concerned drew up fresh programmes within the limits suggested and the proposed allocation was forwarded to the Secretary of State in March 1946.[3]

It is more difficult to discover from the published material concerning development planning in the non-British territories discussed here what has been the extent of the 'departmental' approach to the collection of data. Though, as we shall see, the general impression given is that the investigations have tended to be mainly those of 'problems', the progress reports indicate that at least when dealing with variations in the plans the individual departments have been able to put forward their own data and their own views on a departmental basis without special reference to some inter-departmental tackling of 'problems'. One may surmise that even in the original drafting of the plans there must have been at least some

[1] Cf. *Preliminary Statement on Development Planning in Nigeria*, 1945, paras. 7, 8, 13.
[2] Cf. *Ten Year Plan of Development and Welfare for the Gold Coast*, 1946, pp. 1 and 2.
[3] Cf. The Gambia: *Memorandum on Development*, 1946, para. 2.

mixture of the 'departmental' and the 'problem' approach to the collection of data.

The 'Problem' Approach. The colonial administrative organs—central departments or local administrations—have usually been set up from the point of view of administrative expediency and in accordance with the conditions prevailing in each territory. Thus one single department might deal with health and sanitation, labour, social welfare and prisons. On the other hand, agricultural output might depend upon the Department of Agriculture, the Department of Veterinary Services, the Public Works Department in connection with roads and irrigation, the Department of Rural Water Supplies for wells and the general supply of drinking water for men and animals, the Department of Health, the Department of Trade for supplies of fertilizers and the marketing of products, etc.

Instead of dovetailing development proposals originating in the departments and hence dealing in a fragmentary fashion with some of the main economic or social problems, an attempt has been made in certain cases to define the fields of action first and then to ask all the departments covering parts of such fields to put forward their own views based on the facts known to them, thus leading to what might be called a 'problem' approach to development planning. This approach has been especially characteristic of the Belgian and Netherlands plans as well as, with certain qualifications, of the French plans, and has also been applied in a number of cases in the British territories.

'Justifying' the plan for the development of the Belgian Congo, M. Wigny, Minister for Colonies, pointed out[1] that in an administrative programme everything dovetails, that you cannot lift a link without the whole chain moving. Obviously the metaphor holds good only within certain limits: there are fields where the connection is immediate and close, others where it is fairly loose. M. Wigny's own example, centring on agriculture, takes into account the need for the training of agricultural instructors, for the construction of feeder roads and for the development of local markets. It does not discuss, for example, the impact of anti-malarial measures or of university education or of the provision of hydro-electric power.

The 'chain' tends naturally to be broken down into lengths—i.e. problems (communications, agriculture, housing, education, power, etc.) to be tackled on their own, but with cross-references either on a local or on a country-wide scale.

[1] Cf. *Plan Décennal*, 1949, p. xii.

THE COLLECTION OF DATA

The first ten-year plan in Surinam which made a general survey of needs, local manpower, natural resources and available finance, proceeded to put the emphasis on the immediately productive projects (with agricultural development as the most important problem and industry and forestry as the 'also-rans'). The not immediately productive projects were allocated the 'remainder' of the available funds.[1]

In the French territories, where there has been a much greater emphasis on metropolitan directives, the problem approach seems to have been reached through administrative osmosis. There was a rough emphasis in the first phase on the development of the 'understructure' to deal with the problem of the opening up of the colonies. Large-scale economic enterprises were the fashion in the second phase, to deal with the problem of backwardness by introducing 'modern' features. When it was realized that large-scale economic enterprises were possibly premature, agricultural extension programmes were put forward in an attempt to deal with the problem of rural development and thus to make the best use of the available manpower and natural resources. This third phase is still in force at the time of writing.

In the British territories the problem approach has varied, as may be expected, in emphasis and intensity from case to case. Thus in Tanganyika the Planning Committee appointed sub-committees to consider in fuller detail a number of special problems such as the development of the road system of the territory and the co-ordination of development proposals in regard to agriculture, animal husbandry and soil conservation.[2]

In Sierra Leone it was stated that as the object of the development plan was the improvement of the material welfare of the people in the widest sense along balanced lines, its various aspects were correlated and designed to be of mutual assistance. Thus the improvement of the general health and the standard of living of the population was to be attained by a combination of medical (both curative and preventive), agricultural, veterinary, forestry and fishing schemes, improved food supplies and dietary, town planning, housing and sanitation, water supplies and, in large centres, electricity supplies.[3]

In Mauritius the whole field of development and welfare was

[1] Cf. *Planning the Future of Surinam*, 1953, pp. 6 ff.
[2] Cf. Tanganyika Territory: *An Outline of Post-War Development Proposals*, 1944, para. 7.
[3] Cf. *An Outline of the Ten Year Plan for the Development of Sierra Leone*, 1946, paras. 5 and 6.

surveyed and the sum earmarked for each individual project was determined with a view to completing 'a balanced programme' which should be 'within the colony's financial capacity'.[1]

In North Borneo investigations of problems as opposed to departmental schemes seem to have been largely a matter not of choice but of necessity, the staff position and the pressure of work having been such that only in a few cases had the heads of departments been able to prepare full development schemes. The report was therefore drawn up by a specially appointed Development Secretary, though proposals in the report were discussed with the officials concerned.[2]

In the West Indies, under the influence of the successive Comptrollers and their advisory staff the tendency has on the whole been to concentrate on the problems of development which needed urgent tackling, a tendency which was no doubt facilitated by the very rudimentary administration in existence in each of the many, but small and poor, dependencies and which allowed only of a minimum of departments. But even in the comparatively larger territory of Jamaica the projects examined by the 1945 Development Committee were not only those which had been put forward by 'departments and other authorities'; the reports of a number of committees and individuals who had recently examined important aspects of policy, including particularly the Agricultural Policy Committee and the Economic Policy Committee, were also taken into account.[3]

It is obviously difficult to assert categorically, even after a careful study, that a plan has really been based on the problem—as opposed to the departmental—survey of the needs for future expenditure. It is difficult not to wonder at least whether, for example, the Sierra Leone plan has not succeeded by a careful use of the editorial capacities of the drafting officer in endowing a compilation of departmental schemes with an aura of problem analysis. The alternative to departmental schemes is administratively complicated. The problem analysis involves both the formation of an *ad hoc* committee of specialists, who may not be normally working together, and who would therefore have to meet for a certain amount of time if they are to form themselves into a smoothly working body; and access to information dispersed in a number of departments. Multiply this by the number of problems to be analysed and there will be very few

[1] Cf. *Memorandum on Mauritius Development and Welfare.* Ten Year Plan, 1946, para. 77.
[2] Cf. E. W. Ellison, Development Secretary: *Reconstruction and Development for North Borneo, 1948–55,* 1948.
[3] Cf. *Ten Year Plan of Development for Jamaica,* 1945, para. 11.

colonial territories individually able or inclined to make available the necessary personnel to sit on the committees and, within the departments, to feed the committees with data.

Some territories have attempted an easy way out of this difficulty by appointing, as already mentioned, outside planning experts. A development of this approach can be seen in the more recent planning proposals for Jamaica, Surinam, British Guiana, Nigeria and Malaya made by the International Bank for Reconstruction and Development at the invitation of the respective governments. In all these cases the governments have had to put at the disposal of the investigators or of the investigating missions the existing documentation and in certain cases have had to add a certain amount of further documentation collected at the request of the planners; but they have not been faced with the need for releasing, for purposes both of investigation and of committee work, the very senior officials who would otherwise have been necessary.

(B) CONCERNING RESOURCES

Government resources for development can be classified into: contributions from metropolitan funds; local and external loans; and local resources, usually derived from taxation. Revenue-earning public services such as railway transport, posts and telegraphs, electricity and water supplies seldom even cover their costs to the colonies.

But if the origin of development resources can thus be easily classified, governments have found it very difficult to arrive at even moderately accurate estimates, for planning purposes, of the future size of these resources. Very characteristic in this sense was the reaction of the Barbados Planning Committee to the detailed suggestions made by the Comptroller of Development and Welfare in the West Indies for the estimation of available finance.

The Comptroller, in a memorandum containing 'suggestions for the preparation of development plans', had proposed that the sum available for development purposes should be calculated in the following manner: basic revenue, less basic expenditure on normal services for a typical year; multiplied by ten, because the period of the plan was to be a ten-year one; plus additional revenue obtainable by increased taxation; plus sums that could be raised by loans; plus the Colonial Development and Welfare allocations; plus any sums available from surplus balances.

The Barbados Planning Committee commented that though at first sight this may appear a simple and straightforward calculation, on examination it could be seen that under Barbados conditions it was not really a practicable one. In Barbados, with its one-crop economy, there is really no such thing as basic revenue or basic expenditure on normal services during a typical year.[1]

Other planning committees were less outspoken or possibly less aware of the difficulties involved in these forecasts. But sooner or later they all had to cope with the problems raised by the unreliability of such forecasts.

This unreliability has been chiefly due to the rapid and unforeseen post-war changes in world prices, especially marked in the case of the products of the colonial territories. In the Belgian Congo the price index for exports for 1956 with the 1948–9 average as basis was 144, with partial indices of 175 for mineral exports and 109 for vegetable products. The 1936–8 indices on the same basis were respectively 28, 36 and 20.[2] Rhodesia's original ten-year plan envisaged an expenditure of £5·5 million.[3] Following the rise in the price of raw materials, it proved possible to increase the planned outlay to £13 million in the 1947 Plan, to £17 million in the 1948 Revision, to £36 million in 1951, to £47 million in 1952, and to £52 million in 1953.[4] In Uganda and in the Gold Coast there were similar rapid changes in planned expenditure following increases in income due to high prices for cotton, coffee and cocoa. In most of the colonies, with the possible exception of some of the West Indian territories, the changes in income, though in certain cases comparatively smaller than those already quoted, have still been appreciable.

Costs of development also increased throughout due to increases in the costs of equipment as well as to even larger increases in local wages leading to discrepancies between increases in monetary and in real resources. No attempt has been made so far to estimate absolute or percentage changes in resources in real terms for the colonial territories as a whole, but the general tendency seems to have been towards an increase, though varying in size from territory to territory.

The forecasting of government resources thus tended to prove an impossible task for the administrations concerned, though fortunately for their peace of mind forecasts have tended until recently to err on the low side.

[1] Cf. *Barbados Sketch Plan of Development, 1946–56*, para. 57.
[2] Cf. Banque Centrale du Congo Belge et du Ruanda-Urundi: *Rapport, 1956*, May 1957, Table 1, p. 37.
[3] Cf. Acting Chief Secretary's Minute, SOEC 16 of April 23, 1946, quoted in para. 11 of the *Ten Year Development Plan for Northern Rhodesia*, 1948.
[4] Cf. respective plans and reports.

Attempts to decide how much of these resources would be available for development had to overcome an additional stumbling-block: that of the meaning of the word development. The problem may be outlined as involving a decision on what recurrent costs can be fairly included in development and for how long. How long can an additional teacher be carried under the head of development of educational services and when has he become part of the established educational services so that his pay should therefore be included in the normal expenditure of such services—thus automatically reducing the amount available for development expenditure? One radical solution, now accepted in many territories, of transforming development plans into capital development plans and of including every other type of expenditure in the normal budget side-steps, but does not solve, this problem.

If the existence of independent, income earning and spending, public or semi-public authorities, such as Produce Marketing Boards (not to mention private development expenditure) are also taken into account, there is little wonder that it is in the forecast of resources available for development that many administrations have been most widely out.

CHAPTER 9

The Territorial Governments' Planning Machineries III

PLANNING BODIES

THE description of the first planning stage, that of the administrative gathering of basic material needed for decisions on priorities and for the drawing up of development plans has already necessitated references to the second stage: that of the setting up of planning organizations. It is indeed sometimes difficult to separate the two stages or to say which came first. It is, on the other hand, possible to make some rough distinctions within the second stage between various kinds of planning organizations.

One type of planning organization is that arising naturally from the first stage. The planning committee may in such cases be simply *all the heads of departments* sitting together under the chairmanship of whoever is administratively the senior person, usually in the case of the British territories the Chief Secretary or the Colonial Secretary, or sometimes under the Secretary for Finance.

But such a body, except in the case of very small administrations, could only be very unwieldy. *A restricted committee* has therefore been usually appointed from among the heads of departments to include the heads of the departments most directly concerned in development projects.

Thus in the Gambia the Development Committee, appointed by the Governor in 1941, consisted of the Colonial Secretary as chairman, with the Senior Medical Officer, the Director of Education and the Senior Agricultural Superintendent as members. Close touch was maintained throughout with those government departments and officials who were not represented on the committee but who were concerned in post-war development plans.[1]

In Uganda, as a result of the passing of the Colonial Development and Welfare Act in 1940 a change in the machinery previously existing for the planning and execution of schemes for development and welfare was deemed necessary and a Development and Welfare Committee was created consisting of the Financial Secretary and of

[1] Cf. *Development and Welfare in the Gambia*, June 1943, Introduction, para. 3.

the Directors of Medical Services, of Education and of Agriculture, and under the chairmanship of the Chief Secretary.[1]

In Northern Rhodesia a technical sub-committee of the Native Development Board was appointed, consisting of the Director of Medical Services as chairman and the heads of the African Education, Agriculture and Forestry, and Veterinary Departments as members. In 1945 the Acting Director of Game and Tsetse was added to this committee. The Commissioner of Native Development was secretary. This sub-committee was required to examine development plans.[2]

In Malaya an Economic Development Committee was set up towards the end of 1946 under the chairmanship of the then Economic Adviser and composed of certain heads of departments.[3]

Where the territory concerned has strong regional divisions the Development Committee sometimes includes *regional representatives*.

Thus in Nigeria a Development Branch, under a Development Secretary, was established in the secretariat to work in close touch with a Central Development Board consisting of the Development Secretary as chairman, the three Chief Commissioners representing the three regions, the Financial Secretary, the Commissioner of the Colony, and the Director of Public Works. This Central Development Board was to deal with the general principles of development planning and the policy underlying it and to be the final deciding factor, subject to the approval of the Governor, in regard to overall priorities and the proportionate allocation of the various development activities between one part of the country and another, year by year.[4]

In the Belgian Congo the special secretariat which was established in Leopoldville and which worked in close contact with the heads of departments took into consideration also the views of the provincial administrations within the colony.

In the French territories, where development plans were based chiefly on metropolitan funds, territorial administrations were mainly concerned with putting forward to the central institutions in Paris proposals for the use of such funds. Metropolitan administrators usually favoured proposals which combined detailed territorial estimates with wider, 'federal' or 'supra-federal', conceptions.

[1] Cf. Uganda Protectorate: *Joint Report of the Standing Finance Committee and the Development and Welfare Committee on Post-War Development*, no date of publication, para. 2.
[2] Cf. *Ten Year Development Plan for Northern Rhodesia*, 1948, para. 3.
[3] Cf. *Progress Report of the Development Plan for the Federation of Malaya, 1950–2*, published 1953, p. 1.
[4] Cf. *Ten Year Plan of Development and Welfare for Nigeria*, 1945, para. 33.

A communications network for the federation of French Equatorial Africa meeting possibly also the needs of the Trust Territory of the Cameroons would thus be more favourably regarded than one dealing, say, with the constituent territory of Gabon alone.

In certain territories, especially where the political situation was such that some consultation of persons from outside the administration was considered advisable, the development committees could include also a certain number of *unofficial members*.

Thus in Tanganyika, when it was decided at the end of 1943 to turn to a more detailed consideration of post-war planning, a Development Branch of the secretariat was set up to undertake this process in close collaboration with a planning committee consisting of the heads of departments especially concerned and including unofficial members representing agricultural and economic interests.[1]

But few colonial territories could in the early days of planning have had development committees composed entirely of unofficial members. The Seychelles seems to have been such an exception. The Development Programme Committee, as appointed by His Excellency the Governor on February 13, 1947, comprised the following members: the chairman, five unofficial members of the Legislative Council, and nine members nominated by the Seychelles Taxpayers and Land-owners Association.[2]

The tendency throughout the colonial empires towards an increasing proportion of unofficial members in successive development committees has been quite strong, for obvious reasons connected with the rapid political changes. Especially sweeping in this context are the changes now taking place throughout the French colonies following the Act of June 23, 1956.

In the case of the British colonies the plans drawn up by these territorial planning committees have had to be scrutinized by two more bodies before their final approval for implementation.

One of these bodies is the *Colonial Office*. Its immediate concern has been with the specific ways in which CD & W funds were going to be used under the plan. To enable a proper check both on the planning of CD & W schemes and on their implementation, separate CD & W allocations have normally been made for each definite project, carrying an identification number and subject to yearly accounting. General-purpose grants have on the whole been discouraged.

[1] Cf. Tanganyika Territory. *An Outline of Post-War Development Proposals*, 1944, Introduction, para. 3.
[2] Cf. Seychelles: *Ten Year Development Plan*, 1947, p. 1.

The Colonial Office has also been looking at the plans from a more general point of view. With the help of the wider experience of the experts available to it in London it has tried to keep a proper balance between the various sectors of the whole plan including, but not restricted to, CD & W schemes. This has usually implied correspondence between officials of the local administrations and the Colonial Office or sometimes personal discussions, usually in London.

Thus in the case of Nigeria, when the departmental schemes were completed, the Development Secretary and the Director of Public Works proceeded to England for discussions with the Colonial Office. These discussions lasted some eight weeks, during which time the original plan was re-shaped and re-formed in the light of such information as was available regarding supplies of men and materials. The result was an 'approximate' programme for eleven years, starting with 1945-6 and ending with the financial year 1955-6, and amounting to some £35 million to £40 million. Some of the schemes contained in the plan were sufficiently definite and final for the Secretary of State to accept them as suitable for immediate assistance under the CD & W Act.[1]

The Gambia had to revise its ten-year programme once because its anticipated allocation from CD & W funds was shown in 1945 to have been over-optimistic, and again because after its new proposals were sent to London the assumption on which that allocation had been based—that in the special circumstances of the Gambia such a programme should be weighted on the side of social rather than economic development—was 'no longer considered valid by His Majesty's Government in the United Kingdom'.[2]

And in the case of Sierra Leone, though the Secretary of State considered the outline of the ten-year plan for the development of Sierra Leone to be 'well-balanced and carefully thought out', he suggested that the proposed programme could not be implemented with the funds likely to be available within the period without a considerable expansion of government revenue. As a result, the Government of Sierra Leone did not find it possible to provide detailed estimates of all the work planned for 1947 for consideration in the Estimates in the usual manner. Provision had to be made under a special Head of the Estimates for those schemes which had already received the Secretary of State's approval, with a lump-sum provided for expenditure on other schemes. That lump-sum represented the

[1] Cf. *Preliminary Statement on Development Planning in Nigeria*, 1945, para. 8, 9, 10.
[2] Cf. The Gambia: *Memorandum on Development*, 1946, para. 2.

amount immediately available for development in 1947 from the Sierra Leone Government's own resources and did not take into account any additional assistance obtainable under the CD & W Act.[1]

As already mentioned in the section dealing with the metropolitan governments' planning, this type of checks, controls and advice by the Colonial Office applied throughout the British colonial territories, though it was obviously the more important the greater, relatively or absolutely, the contributions of CD & W funds to the financing of development plans. In a territory where the plan involved a comparatively small amount of money, most of which came from CD & W funds, the Colonial Office views tended to be paramount. They were also very weighty in a case like Nigeria, where, though the CD & W funds did not constitute a major proportion of the plan, the plan itself was so large that the absolute contribution was appreciable. It is only in the cases in which the CD & W contribution was fairly small both relatively and absolutely that the Colonial Office influence was least felt, as in Northern Rhodesia and in the Gold Coast.

A second body to be consulted in most of the British territories before the development plans could be implemented has been the local *Legislative Council*, or some similar consultative or legislative body. Such consultation has tended to be a purely formal affair, though there have been certain interesting exceptions to the rule, such as in the case of Trinidad and Tobago. A rapid development towards self-government has not necessarily made the direct influence of a Legislative Assembly debate more effective, the system of majority government on the United Kingdom pattern but within a local framework usually ensuring the acceptance of the Government's plan, sometimes without any modification by the Assembly.

For the *French territories* the formal decision-making body has been the *Comité Directeur* of FIDES, a composite body under the chairmanship of the Minister for Overseas France and which includes, besides the heads of FIDES, of CCFOM and of the *Commissariat Général au Plan*, also members of the French Parliament, of the Assembly of the French Union, and representatives of the participating administrations and organisations. (CCFOM includes also representatives of private interests.) The development proposals put forward by the individual territories, as processed by the relevant sections of the Ministry for Overseas France, have been the basis for discussion within the *Comité Directeur*. Though the ultimate responsibility for decisions has been that of the *Comité Directeur*,

[1] Cf. Sierra Leone: *Progress Report on the Development Programme for the year 1946*, 1947, para. 2.

PLANNING BODIES

the proposals as received from the Ministry have been usually accepted without appreciable alterations. This relationship is changing appreciably with the inauguration of self-government throughout the French overseas territories. The ultimate decisions are now made by the territorial governments and the *Comité Directeur* withdraws increasingly into the rôle of adviser as exercised by the British Colonial Office since the introduction of the CD & W Fund system. The much greater reliance of the French territories on metropolitan funds will nevertheless continue to be reflected in a more widespread consultation by the territorial governments of the experts of FIDES, CCFOM and of the other overseas authorities in Paris.

The metropolitan impact on the *Belgian Congo* development plans is of a rather different character. There is no need for a powerful centralized authority in Brussels, as the Congo and the contiguous Ruanda-Urundi, the only Belgian territories involved, are fully able to 'centralize' their problems locally. Nor are there any Belgian public funds involved in the Congo development plans, though some funds, mainly of the budget subsidy type, are provided by the metropolitan government in the case of the over-populated and comparatively poor trust territory of Ruanda-Urundi. Belgian Congo loans raised on the Brussels and other markets have of course the backing and the expert advice of the Belgian Government. But certain major policy decisions, especially in connection with the possibility of participation of foreign capital in development projects (such as that of the Inga power development scheme) have aroused a certain amount of political controversy in Belgium. A revision of educational policies for the natives as well as a liberalization of political conditions may also become matters for decision by the metropolitan government. Such changes of policy would have repercussions in the colonial plans both concerning the relative weights between the sectors and the future emphasis within each sector. Not only could, say, agriculture get a greater share, but native agriculture may be allocated a larger proportion than before compared to the Belgian immigrants.

In the case of *Surinam*, the only rôle of the Netherlands Government has been that of the provision of funds and of experts. Discussions concerning the funds as a whole as well as the broad fields of expenditure have taken place, but at 'Government level', in accordance with the 'dominion' status Surinam attained late in 1954. The influence of the Netherlands advisory mission (established in 1955) in the selection and the scope of individual projects seems nevertheless to have been appreciable.

CHAPTER 10

The Territorial Governments' Planning Machineries IV

IMPLEMENTATION OF THE PLAN

WHETHER the plan has been drawn up on the basis of a compilation of departmental reports or whether it is the result of some *ad hoc* planning body outside the departments, one obvious way of proceeding to the third stage, that of implementation, is to use the existing administrative channels.

A preliminary condition for such implementation is the existence of at least some detailed development schemes. In practice, in the first development plans most of such schemes fell either in the category financed directly from metropolitan government grants, such as CD & W schemes or FIDES projects, or in that of detailed individual schemes put forward as part of the departmental plans and which had been accepted unchanged.

The proportion of such schemes within a plan differs appreciably from territory to territory. Thus in the Gold Coast, where the first ten-year plan was in fact a summary of departmental projects for a number of years ahead, the first years involved simply the completion of departmental works already in hand or already planned in detail; the Public Works Department, the Department of Rural Water Supplies, the Railway and Harbour Authority, the Department of Education, etc., continued their work without being greatly affected by the almost theoretical existence of a plan. Variations, usually in the sense of delays in their plans, did occur but were due to lack of staff or equipment.[1]

In the cases in which major readjustments of the departmental plans had, on the other hand, to be undertaken at some stage during the drafting of the plan there has been need for new detailed study by the departments concerned of the changed projects. In Nigeria, for example, there were a number of schemes sufficiently definite and at the same time acceptable—such as the development of rural and

---

[1] Cf. *A Ten Year Plan of Development and Welfare for the Gold Coast*, 1946, especially memoranda by Heads of Departments; and cf. *Progress Report on the Draft Ten Year Plan of Development and Welfare for the Period Ended 31st December*, 1949, 1950.

urban water supplies, the expansion of the road system and of telecommunications, electrical development, and anti-malarial measures for the Lagos area—for the respective departments to be able to undertake them immediately with the help of CD & W funds approved by London.[1] The major reshaping of the plan through the discussions already mentioned between the Nigerian administration and the Colonial Office implied, on the other hand, reshaping of many of the individual items, necessitating even the setting up of a new department—the Department of Commerce and Industries.[2]

The existence of a final, overall plan as well as of detailed schemes within the plan are only the necessary prerequisites for its implementation. To ensure its application there must be, in addition, some control over the implementing authorities.

Such control in terms of the plan has been quite close in the case of the French, Belgian and Netherlands territories. In the case of the French and, to some extent, of the Netherlands territories this control has been exercised through the specially-set-up organizations for the disbursement of funds and has involved a close check for the prevention of unauthorized virements. In the case of the Belgian territories monthly progress reports for internal administrative consumption in terms of the plan; the comparative absence of outside 'political' pressures in favour of variations in the established plan; the obvious determination of the administration to carry out the stated programme in terms both of the plan's main objectives and of its agreed time-table, have ensured a fairly close conformity with the physical programme if not with its financial aspects. In the British territories the position has been much less clearcut. The measures taken to ensure conformity with the plan have varied both as between territories and within the same territory in accordance with changes in views and problems, providing for the student an almost complete coverage of all possible variations on the theme.

FINANCIAL CONTROL

In the first stages, at least, of the implementation of the plans the normal procedure of annual budgeting has usually been considered sufficient in many of the British territories to ensure that the schemes approved were carried out within the limits of the available finance and of the available men and materials. In some cases, like that of the Gold Coast, no specific financial authority was set up to exercise

[1] Cf. *Preliminary Statement on Development Planning in Nigeria*, 1945, para. 10.
[2] Cf. *op. cit.*, paras. 13, 17 *et al.*

control over the first plan. It is difficult to discover whether there was even any kind of informal supervision, possibly through the transmogrification of the Financial Secretary into a watch-dog over the plan.

In other cases, like Sarawak or Nigeria, where some development secretariat or a similar organization was set up under a not very senior officer, it can only be surmised that if departmental activities were kept close to the plan it must have been done through the annual allocations for development purposes, but there is little published evidence of this.

In certain territories a more conscious effort was made from the beginning to ensure a close conformity of departmental activities to the plan. The simplest method evolved was that of financial allocation and control exercised on the basis of the plan's estimates.

This qualification must be introduced because in every administration some financial control is always exercised, but there is usually no established yard-stick, outside the yearly bargaining between departments for the available resources, by which expenses can be allocated. The existence of a plan does not, unless there is a will to conform to it, automatically transform the annual bargaining process into an agreed long-range programme of priorities. The plan can simply become a statement of intentions as at the time of drafting without any undertaking that such intentions will not vary, sometimes appreciably, over the so-called period of the plan. Thus the acceptance of some financial control in terms of the plan is the first real indication of the willingness and earnestness of the various administrative departments to implement the plan as agreed upon at the moment of drafting.

Development Reports. A useful step towards ensuring that the financial provisions of the plan are carried out is the establishment and publication of separate annual accounts for expenditures under the plan. This can be done by the annual publication of a progress report. Such a report would include a statement of works undertaken in the previous year and an estimate of the works to be undertaken during the following and succeeding years to the end of the planning period. It would also compare results with the original estimates of the plan and would include an explanation of the reasons for any variations which might have occurred.

Such a progress report was, of course, one of the conditions for the granting of money by His Majesty's Government under CD & W schemes, but it only applied strictly to such schemes. Its extension to cover the whole development plan was not always immediate or permanent, nor did it necessarily cover annual budgetary periods. In addition, the publication of progress reports often tended to be delayed appreciably due both to shortages of staff for the compilation of the individual departmental reports and to printing delays.

Thus in the British territories which presented separate reports of development the Northern Rhodesia Development Authority published in 1950 a report covering the period from June 1948 to December 1949, and including the plans for 1950, followed afterwards by annual reports. Kenya published a Development and Reconstruction Authority Report covering the period August 1, 1945, to December 31, 1946, and afterwards annual reports. The Gold Coast published its first progress report on the 1946 Plan in 1950 covering the period until December 31, 1949, the accounting difference between the April to March budgetary year and the January to December Development Report making comparisons and checks rather difficult. Development progress reports for the second development plan starting in 1952 were therefore changed to coincide with the budgetary year. The Gambia published its report on development for 1950–2 in 1953; and for Sierra Leone the last progress report available in the Colonial Office Library is that referring to 1949.

Development Budgets. Another measure which has proved useful in ensuring that priorities established under development plans are adhered to has been the introduction of special development budgets.

Such a separate development budget was introduced in Tanganyika in 1947 and was voted on at the same time as the normal territorial budget, though the development plan itself had not yet been approved.[1] Later on, and in the light of further experience, this original development budget underwent a series of modifications. In 1952 a portion of the recurrent expenditure from the development plan was absorbed in the territorial budget, and in 1953 the budget was divided into three parts: Part I, containing the recurrent departmental Estimates; Part II, containing the projects financed from the Agricultural Development Reserve; and Part III, confined to capital works.[2] In Kenya the colony's 1946 Estimates were divided into two parts, the first devoted to ordinary government revenue and expenditure, and the second part comprising the revenue and expenditure

[1] Cf. Tanganyika Territory: *Report for the year 1947.*
[2] Cf. *Development Plan 1955–60*, 1955, Capital Works Programme, para. 5.

relating to development and reconstruction. It was hoped by this division to provide the general public with a clearer picture of the Government's intentions.[1]

Development Funds. Two more definite steps to ensure that the expenditure of the departments is in accordance with the provision of the plan have been the creation of a separate development fund, and the establishment of some body directly entrusted with the supervision of the plan.

Both these steps have usually had certain additional justifications and purposes, often expounded upon at length by their protagonists. The fund has also been a device for ensuring the continued availability of the resources necessary for carrying out the plan, and the supervisory body has also been a revising body, reallocating priorities in accordance with changed conditions.

Thus in Kenya, in order, as explained by the Government, to ensure that DARA might be free as far as possible from uncertainty in regard to the amount of money available to undertake the programme of development and reconstruction to be assigned to it, an uncertainty rendered inevitable by the normal system of colonial estimating for an annual balanced budget, the Government decided to establish a Development and Reconstruction Fund into which all moneys earmarked for capital expenditure on development and reconstruction over a period of years would be paid. The intention was that moneys once paid into this fund could not be diverted to non-development purposes and that the amount available would be largely independent of the normal fluctuations in the colony's annual revenue and expenditure.

In Mauritius the stated primary object of the separation of the development budget from the ordinary budget was to ensure that the programme of development could be entered upon with some asurance that it would be carried out irrespective of the fluctuations in the colony's revenue due to its dependence on primary products. It was hoped that the establishment of a Mauritius Development and Welfare Fund, to which were to be carried the moneys earmarked for development and from which expenditure on approved projects was to be periodically voted by the legislature, with no automatic lapse at the end of the financial year, would enable a comprehensive programme to be planned and executed. The fund would also assist the colony to break away from a policy, sporadic in its application and largely ineffective in its results, of promoting development schemes

[1] Cf. DARA: *Report*, 1947, para. 5.

only in prosperous years and slowing down or abandoning them in years of adversity.

It was also considered important that accumulated reserves should be carried to the fund and spent on long-range plans designed to bring lasting benefit to the colony rather than that they should be the object of annual raids designed to fortify annual budgets which should normally be balanced. Accordingly it was agreed that the fund should be opened by a substantial transfer from surplus funds accumulated during the war and the necessary provision was made in the Estimates for 1946–7.

In addition, by the adoption of this procedure it was felt that the Council of Government and the public could obtain a clear idea of what was proposed in the way of development and welfare in the following years, and that the officers charged with the execution of the projects included and to be included in the plan would be stimulated by the knowledge that there was going to be continuity of effort and a planned objective.[1]

The development-fund technique can, of course, be abused. In the Gold Coast development funds proliferated until there were three main development funds under the direct control of the Government, as well as a Cocoa Marketing Board Fund, an Industrial Development Fund and an Agricultural Development Fund, under the respective controls of the Cocoa Marketing Board, the Industrial Development Corporation and the Agricultural Development Corporation, all three of which were undertaking development projects.

Similar specialized development funds were set up in a number of other territories usually as a result of produce marketing-board activities, as in the case of the Farmers' Fund in the Gambia and of the various produce marketing boards' funds in Nigeria; and in at least one case, that of Uganda, it actually forced the Government into a change of policy concerning its treatment of 'development' and 'normal' expenditure.

In 1948 the Uganda Government was still maintaining that while 'development is naturally a permanent feature of the ultimate harbour', the day-to-day expenditure on normal activities was at least as important a feature of the course to be followed in reaching it; in other words, that it was impossible in practice to separate development from normal expenditure.

This view had been further strengthened by the discovery that the reason for which the cost of carrying the first development plan into

[1] Cf. *Memorandum on Mauritius Development and Welfare, Ten Year Plan*, 1946, paras. 1, 2, 3.

effect was proving to be much greater than had originally been estimated was not connected with specific development schemes, but with what was termed in the plan 'normal' expansion—that is to say, with the cost of carrying on the normal day-to-day activities of government.

As a result of this discovery it had been decided to integrate completely the cost of development with that of maintaining the existing activities of government, to break down the resulting figures into programmes showing when and on what objects it was proposed that expenditure should be incurred in each of the remaining eight years of the decennium covered by the plan, and to reclassify the figures under heads of account so as to facilitate comparison with those in the annual Estimates.[1]

But within two years this 'complete integration' of the cost of development with the cost of maintaining the existing activities of government had to be abandoned. The world prices obtained for Uganda cotton and coffee had come to exceed the guaranteed sums paid to the growers by so much that the Cotton and Coffee Price Assistance Funds, which were the repositories of that excess, had rapidly mounted to sums greater than it was felt prudence against possible bad seasons required. It was therefore decided in 1951 to close the Cotton Price Assistance Fund at £20 million and to pay over the excess then and in the future into a specially created African Development Fund. That decision, which made some £15 million immediately available for African development over and above what had been envisaged in the Harris Plan, was thus a complete *volte-face*.[2]

There were, of course, territories such as Tanganyika and Sierra Leone which continued throughout to finance their development projects through yearly budgets without the help of special local funds, their only separate budgeting being concerned with the funds supplied under the CD & W schemes.

SUPERVISORY AUTHORITIES

The supervisory authorities specially established to ensure the implementation of the plans differ widely in their main features. They may be simply the original Development Planning Committee, whose duties were defined to include those of a supervisory body.

[1] Cf. *1948 Revision of a Development Plan for Uganda* (also known as the Harris Plan), 1949, paras. 3, 4.
[2] Cf. *A Five Year Capital Development Plan, 1955–60*, 1954, para. 3.

IMPLEMENTATION OF THE PLAN

In Tanganyika it was thus decided at the beginning of 1946 to remove the detailed work of preparing plans and other matters connected with development from direct association with the Secretariat and to transfer responsibility for such matters to a separate organization which could pay undivided attention to them. In accordance with that policy a Development Commission was appointed. Its main functions were to maintain close contact with the manner in which development projects were being executed; to ensure as far as possible that the work was being expeditiously carried out; and to deal as occasion arose with matters which appeared to be impeding progress. As its first task the Commission was asked to 'draw up a general and comprehensive plan of development and welfare for the territory, covering a ten-year period'.[1]

But it was on the whole more usual to consider the justification for the existence of the Development Planning Committee as finished with the completion of the plan and to appoint a new body for the supervision of its implementation.

Thus, as we have seen, in Kenya DARA was established to be responsible to the Governor for the expenditure of all capital and other sums specifically allocated for development and reconstruction purposes and for the co-ordinated execution of approved development and reconstruction plans.[2] In Uganda a Development Section of the secretariat under a specially appointed Development Commissioner was set up in July 1947 to deal entirely with development projects. In Northern Rhodesia a Development Authority was established in 1947 to be responsible to the Government for the carrying out of development plans (as approved in the Legislative Council) in so far as staff, materials and other considerations would permit. It was to control all development funds, including loans, authorized by the Legislative Council for expenditure in the course of each three-year period which would be placed under requisition. Its membership was set at two Officials and two Unofficials.[3]

[1] Cf. *A Ten Year Development and Welfare Plan for Tanganyika Territory*, 1946, paras. 2, 3.
[2] Cf. *Sessional Paper No. 3*, 1945, 'Proposals for the Reorganization of the Administration of Kenya.'
[3] Cf. *Northern Rhodesia Ten Year Development Plan*, 1948, para. 27.

CHAPTER 11

The Territorial Governments' Planning Machineries V

REVISING BODIES

WITH the rapidly changing conditions in the immediate post-war period, both from the point of view of income and of costs, the supervisory bodies soon saw themselves forced to act as revising bodies of the existing plan. In the case of Tanganyika this had been specifically foreseen when the first development committee had been set up but in other cases only the need for determining short-term priorities had really been envisaged. The supervisory bodies as set up were not suited for basic replanning and sooner or later, but certainly before the end of the original plan as foreseen at the time of drafting, the fourth stage was reached and new planning committees had to be constituted.

In the British territories, in accordance with the suggestions received from the Secretary of State in 1945, development plans were usually intended to cover a period of ten years, of which only the first five were to be covered in some detail. Ten years was the first planning period envisaged also in the French, Belgian and Netherlands territories. It may therefore have seemed obvious that a second planning committee might have to be appointed before the end of the ten-year period to draw up the next plan if a system of planning were to be continued. In the case of the British and French territories, where detailed plans had only been attempted for the first half of each period, it would indeed have been expected that planning committees would have to be set up much sooner. In the case of Britain the Secretary of State's pronouncements in Parliament in favour of the 1940 recommendations of the Royal Commission for the West Indies that a twenty-year development period was necessary to ensure a future healthy economic situation for the West Indies should have furthermore left no doubt that the ten-year plans being drafted after 1945 in the British territories were regarded in London only as a first instalment of development. But whether this view had not really percolated to the territorial administrations (even the specially appointed Comptroller for the West Indies, for example, was not aware of this point of view until 1942, when he complained to the

Colonial Office of his difficulties in planning ahead in matters like education and agricultural development because his time limit had been set at 1950 by the expiry of the current CD & W Act of 1940) or whether ten or even five years seemed to the administrations to be such a far-off date that it could be left to take care of itself; whatever the reason, there was rarely any specific provision made within the first plan for a second planning committee. One exception was the already quoted case of Tanganyika, where an attempt was made to establish one single permanent body to draft the first plan, supervise its implementation, revise it, and prepare the next plan. The other was Mr Worthington's Uganda development plan, in which the impossibility of planning accurately ahead for more than a very short period, such as of two to three years, and hence the need for the immediate appointment of a revising and replanning body, was very emphatically stated. Mr Worthington was of course perfectly right. None of the territories' plans remained unchanged for more than a very short period—shorter even, in the case of Uganda, than his original two or three years, as he himself pointed out in the annexe to his published plan, which he had to add only a few months after his first draft.

But more often than not such adjustments as were needed were made automatically through the relative capacities of individual departments to fulfil their share of the plan, and through the annual budgets. Specially appointed annual revising bodies, even when set up, often could not be much more than recording bodies of changes outside their control.

It is not easy to say when and for what reason the changes in the plans led in each case to an awareness of the need for a complete recasting of priorities. In certain cases, such as the Gold Coast and Uganda, the unexpectedly rapid rise in revenues, due to increases in world prices of raw materials, made the original plans look very tame, and with a new estimate of both costs and resources a new shift in priorities became important. In others, such as Northern Rhodesia and Nyasaland, increased costs and resources were taken care of by a number of general or partial revisions until it finally became evident that the process could not go on indefinitely. Political developments, as in the Gold Coast and Nigeria, or emergencies as in the case of Kenya and Malaya, also made new planning bodies necessary, adjustments having become so important as to alter completely the original plans. Changes in the executive personnel seem also to have had something to do with decisions on the establishment of new development committees. But though it is not easy to indicate which is the straw that broke the camel's back and at which exact point it broke it, in practically every case a new camel had to be provided at some date during the first planning period.

These new planning committees have tended to differ in two main respects from their predecessors. In the first place the experience of the first planning period led most of the territories to the conclusion that the drafting of a plan is not sufficient if there is no follow-up in the sense of continuous check and revision. Hence, for example, in Kenya it was recommended in the *1951 Report of the Planning Committee* that the committee should be kept in being or that a new committee should be appointed to keep the situation under review and to redefine the targets from time to time as may be required. This committee was to run in parallel with DARA, which had the complementary job of assigning priorities of execution as between works and projects approved.[1] The Development Board appointed in Sarawak in May 1951 was entrusted with the revision of the existing development plan in the light of changing circumstances and prepared the 1955–60 Development Plan.[2] The tendency has thus been towards a standing joint development and supervisory committee.

In the second place, non-officials have become increasingly important as policy-makers. Such a tendency has been strongest where there has been an elected legislature, especially when some of the members of the Government were themselves unofficial members of this legislature. In such cases a separate authority for planning and supervision was less and less acceptable and the planning committee had sooner or later to become a mixed body of official and unofficial members of the new political system and to be under the direct control of the Government and the legislature. 'Development' had either to come under a new department or under a minister, as in Kenya or in the Gold Coast, or else an inter-ministerial, or joint ministerial-and-official, committee had to be set up to advise the Government on problems of development and to approve the new plans or the revision of the old plan to be presented to the legislatures.

The planning machinery has thus been enlarged to take into account additional aspects of the planning problems in the sense that public opinion, or what the political representatives might think is the public's opinion, has to take its place in a much more emphatic manner among the planning considerations than tended to be the

---

[1] Cf. *1951 Report of the Planning Committee*, para. 34.
[2] Cf. *Revised Development Plan of Sarawak, 1951–7*, 1952, pp. 6, 7; *Development Plan of Sarawak*, 1954, p. ii.

case when the planners were exclusively administrators, or even when they included appointed unofficial members.

It was still possible, for example, in 1947 in Sierra Leone to say (after stating that the programme outlined by officials had been 'accepted locally') that the disappointment which had been expressed that greater provision had not been made for social services and for medical and educational improvements in particular was due to the fact that the need for sound economic development in order to sustain and develop social services had not been at first 'readily recognized' by some people who had advocated the expenditure of large sums on these services at the expense of the less spectacular, but essential, economic projects, but that that 'attitude' was now 'changing'.[1]

In contrast, the Gold Coast Development Plan (1951), put forward immediately after the assumption of power by the first Government with an African-elected majority, made a radical change as compared to the officially drafted programme of 1950, increasing the provisions for education in accordance with what the new Government considered to be the public feeling in the country.

In Kenya, as already mentioned, both the Standing Planning Committee and DARA were abolished in 1952 and were replaced by a sub-committee of the Executive Council (with mixed political and administrative membership) to act as a planning body and by the normal ministerial system for the control and implementation of the plan.

THE NEED FOR MORE DETAILED BASIC DATA

The drafting of the first plans had already made it obvious that there was need for much more statistical information than was available at the time. The very rapid changes in incomes and costs which made it necessary to revise the development plans at frequent intervals strengthened the need for such kind of information and in addition made it obvious that there was need also for additional information concerning economic and social relationships within the groups covered by the plans. Increasingly great weight has therefore been placed on the development of statistical organizations within the administrative machinery.

The first major aim of these organizations has been to build up national income and expenditure accounts, if possible on a sector basis. Certain preliminary attempts made along these lines by

[1] Cf. Sierra Leone: *Progress Report on the Development Programme*, 1947, para. 4.

individual experts brought in from outside have suffered greatly from large gaps in the basic information available. Their main virtue may well have been the indication of such gaps to the permanent statistical organizations within the territories concerned.

Thus, discussing the 'steps in planning', the Kenya *Development Programme, 1954–7*, after mentioning a number of investigations, mainly of a technical character, necessary for preparing development programmes stated that economic surveys as opposed to surveys of resources—that is to say to technical and physical surveys—are 'also important'. Such economic surveys were classified in the development programme into two groups, namely surveys of economic institutions ('for development can occur only if appropriate institutions exist') and surveys which take stock of the community's resources; and the need for national income accounts 'which show summarily how the national income is produced, distributed and spent' was emphasized.[1]

Under the British system the territorial statistical organizations, being bodies of experts dealing with problems similar throughout the colonial territories, have found it much easier than most of the other organizations involved in colonial planning to exchange information on their work and, with the help of the statistical division in the Colonial Office and of the staff movements of statisticians between the various territories, there has been some tendency towards the build-up of a common approach to methods and priorities.

[1] Cf. Kenya: *The Development Programme, 1954–7*, p. 3, para. 8.

PART V

ANALYSIS OF THE PLANS

CHAPTER 12

Planning Periods, Resources and Priorities

THE plans, the ways in which they have been implemented, and their effects, are the result of the interaction between the planning machineries established by the various administrations concerned and the economic and social facts with which the respective administrations have had to deal. As the economic and social facts or the administrative set-ups have changed, so have the ways of dealing on a planned basis with the problems of development. An analysis of territorial plans and of their implications which would take such historical changes into consideration could only be undertaken on an individual basis, territory by territory. To avoid the tediousness of such a fragmentary analysis planned development will be broken down into its component stages and each stage will be discussed and illustrated in terms of the relevant territorial plans.

PLANNING PERIODS

Ten-year Plans. The Royal West India Commission recommended in 1940 that for a period of twenty years the sum of £1 million a year should be assured to the West Indies as a contribution from the United Kingdom Government's Exchequer. The United Kingdom, while accepting the principle of this recommendation, did not feel entitled to engage the responsibility of future governments over such a long period and decided therefore to ask Parliament in 1940 to undertake the financial obligations under the CD & W Act for a period of only ten years. When, in 1945, with the end of the war in sight, it was decided to revise the CD & W Act in the light both of the first five years' experience and of the changed circumstances, a ten-year period, 1946–56, was again allowed for. Thus this compromise between the recommendations of the Royal West India Commission and the political traditions and realities of the United Kingdom may have been the main reason for the ultimate concentration on a ten-year period throughout the British Empire and possibly, in imitation of their British precursors, for the first, ten-year, post-war French, Belgian and Netherlands' plans.

Neither the 1940 Act nor the Colonial Office instructions issued under the Act had actually asked for long-term territorial plans for any definite period. Mr MacDonald had indeed mentioned with approval, in June 1939, during the debates in the committee on Supply, that the Governments of Trinidad and Northern Rhodesia had 'given examples of the spirit which animates colonial governments today' by working out and getting accepted by their legislatures five-year plans of social and economic development.[1] But the provisions of the 1940 Act which did not allow of any carry-over of unspent funds from year to year tended to over-emphasize the importance of year-by-year planning. The Secretary of State, when he said that if some queries about certain provisions of the plans were to be raised by the Colonial Office with the colonial governments concerned it was expected that the colonial governments would let the Colonial Office have their views on such queries 'with regard to plans of development for the following year',[2] also seems to have had in mind that detailed planning, at least, would be of the year-by-year type.

Whatever the intentions concerning planning periods in the Colonial Office, the fall of France and the war situation in general led to a postponement of most attempts at any comprehensive planning, and individual plans put forward before 1945 tended to cover planning schemes of possibly definite magnitude but on the whole indefinite periods.[3] Thus Jamaica 'had already been enabled to carry out many important schemes' by the financial assistance granted under the 1940 Act, but it was only the increase in the total sum provided and the lengthening of the period of assistance arising from the 1945 Act which 'made it essential' to work out a long-term plan, which the pressure of war conditions and the shortage of materials and trained staff had previously made impossible.[4]

The changes brought in by the 1945 Act, by the Colonial Paper No. 3 on Development Planning which preceded the 1945 Act, and especially by the Colonial Office circular despatch of November 12, 1945 (published as *Cmd 6713*), sent by the new Labour Colonial Secretary Mr Hall, were almost dramatic. Planning committees proliferated and ten-year plans, until then sporadic, began to be drafted

---

[1] Cf. *Hansard*, June 7, 1939, col. 441.
[2] Cf. *Hansard*, May 21, 1940, col. 120.
[3] E.g. *Development and Welfare in the Gambia*, 1943.
[4] Cf. *A Ten Year Plan of Development for Jamaica*, 1946, para. 11.

throughout the colonial empire. Even though quite a few of these ten-year plans had to be radically redrafted within a very short space of time, due to a large extent to a rapidly changing economic situation, the new drafts also usually kept to the ten-year planning period. Such long term 'planning' was made easier by the arrangements through which, on instruction from the Colonial Office, attempts at detailed planning were made only for the first five years and only some indication of possible expenditure of a fairly vague nature were given for the second five years.

A variation on the ten-year theme was made by some of the latecomers in the planning field who tended to plan with the end of the CD & W Act in mind. Thus North Borneo presented its Reconstruction and Development Plan for the 1948–55 period, and the 1949 Draft Development Plan for the Federation of Malaya covered a six-year period from 1950 to 1955.

Short Plans: Variable Periods. With the experience of the initial development plans behind them an increasing number of territories came to the conclusion that attempts at planning over such a long period as ten years is unrealistic. As a result there has been in the latter stages of colonial planning endeavours a shortening of the period of planning.

In the British territories, where attempts at unified centralized planning by the metropolitan government have been avoided, there has been a great deal of diversification in planning periods in accordance with local needs, problems and views.

Kenya put forward a three-and-a-half-year (1954–7) development programme. Uganda, which, exceptionally among colonial territories, had drafted its first ten-year development plan as early as 1943, and had to have it radically revised at repeated intervals, had a new ten-year plan drawn up in 1946, which was revised and transformed into an eight-year plan in 1948; its next planning period was cut down to five years to coincide with the extension of the CD & W Act. Tanganyika also limited its latest plans to the same five years, 1955 to 1960, obviously for similar reasons. Sarawak's *Revised Development Plan* ran from 1951 to 1957 and then from 1955 to 1960. The Federation of Rhodesia and Nyasaland has put forward a three-year, 1954 to 1957 plan, and has revised it into a 1955–9 plan. Both Northern Rhodesia and Nyasaland, while not drawing up a new plan, have revised their old plans continuously and, by keeping to the same final date, have in fact also continuously shortened the period of planning ahead. Nigeria brought in a revised plan, 1951–6, and an 'Economic Programme', 1955–60. The Gold Coast kept to the ten-year period for its first three plans in 1947, 1950 and 1951, but its detailed planning has covered varying and much shorter periods. Similar methods, leading to *de facto* changes in planning periods, have been applied in the majority of territories.

The general tendency today seems to be for five-year plans to coincide more or less with the foreseen end of the CD & W periods, which, by repeated extensions since 1940, have tended to run in about five-year periods, but with the proviso that major adjustments might be made within that period.

In the French territories, on the other hand, planning periods, which are not connected with the five-year prolongations of the periods of allocation of central funds, are tending to settle down formally to a four-year cycle. The first stage of the 1948 Pleven Plan was completed in 1952. Development projects were continued until 1954 on a year-to-year basis, while the planning committees for the second stage, which soon became in fact a new plan, were set up, presented their plans and had them approved. The new plan was drawn up to cover the period 1954–7 inclusive. The next planning period will probably cover the year 1958–61 inclusive.

Interim Plans. With a succession of plans there is the additional problem of finding the best solution, in terms of planning periods, to the need for transition from one plan to the next. This problem does not seem to have been fully appreciated at first and the end of the first planning period has been reached in certain cases without any definite plans ready for the second planning period. Even in the case of the so-called ten-year plans, as the detailed planning has tended to cover only the first five years, and as even those detailed plans have sometimes been completed, at least in certain of their aspects, before the end of the five years, the administrations have seen themselves fairly quickly faced with a planless gap, to be coped with by some kind of a 'transitional' plan of varying length. The already quoted French experience is one example. Similar transitional periods have also been introduced in many British territories, as in Uganda between 1951 and 1955,[1] in Kenya between 1952 and 1954,[2] in Nigeria— the 'Interim Development Plan'—from 1955 to 1956, and in the Gold Coast since 1956. In Uganda and Kenya, though some pretence was made at the time that the previous plans were still continuing, 'planning' was in fact being done by annual decisions and sometimes even

[1] Cf. *A Five Year Capital Development Plan for Uganda*, 1955–60, paras. 4, 5.
[2] Cf. *Development Programme 1954–7*, paras. 22, 23, 24, 25.

by separate decisions taken at various times within the year. In Uganda major planning decisions on railway extensions, African education, co-operative development, African housing and mechanized farming were thus taken at odd intervals during that transitional period, so that it would be impossible to decide what the planning 'period' has been; and in Kenya similar *ad hoc* decisions were taken through the normal government machinery. In other cases some overlapping of planning periods has been resorted to so as to ensure a smooth transition.

PLANNING RESOURCES

CD & W *Funds.* It has been shown that throughout most of the British territories the movement towards a development plan has been the result of a double incentive: the promise of an allocation from the CD & W funds of 1940 and 1945 as a carrot and, as a related and very fatherly stick, the request for plans from the Colonial Secretaries. In 1940 this was a restricted request, applying only to the CD & W funds. In 1945 it became more sweeping, calling for overall development plans into which the CD & W allocations could be fitted. The CD & W funds were therefore the first resources to be taken into consideration by the territorial authorities when envisaging development plans. Indeed, in certain cases they seem to have been practically the only resources on which plans were based. Such is the case with quite a few of the poorer territories, especially among the small dependencies in certain parts of the West Indies.

Thus in Antigua the (unpublished) 1948 Development Plan seems to have been mainly composed of proposals for the spending of CD & W money.[1] The same considerations seem to have applied to British Honduras, where the 1945 allocation of £600,000, the Evans Commission allocation of £850,000 and the Development Plan Part II (1952–5) allocation of £800,000 provided practically the whole of the capital expenditure for the first development plans, and where even the 1955–60 development expenditure, estimated at some £3·2 million, is to find only about 3 per cent of the total funds from local revenue, and a further 6 per cent from loans, the rest of some 90 per cent being derived from grants. North Borneo at the time of its first 'plan' was living on British Treasury grants and had no reserve funds, little likelihood of raising any loans and its tax-raising capacities were limited by monopolies and restrictive agreements which were a legacy from the Chartered Company days.[2] It was felt in

[1] Cf. *Antigua Development Plans,* para. 9.
[2] Cf. *Reconstruction and Development Plan for North Borneo,* 1948.

Sarawak that even recurrent costs arising from development schemes financed from the CD & W funds could only be met, for at least the initial five-year period, by allocations under the schemes themselves.[1] The Gambia development schemes were almost entirely dependent on CD & W funds, which by 1951 amounted to £1·5 million as compared to a locally-built-up Farmers' Fund, of some £200,000, which was intended to be used for 'such projects as are deemed beneficial to the farming community'.[2]

In other British territories CD & W funds have had a much smaller share in the total development plans. The greatly increased world prices for raw materials after the war, and especially after Korea, led to a rapid increase in the national incomes and in the government revenues of some of the raw materials exporting territories. This increase was given an additional fillip by the devaluation of the pound in 1949. As a result the originally allocated sums under the CD & W Act have sometimes become almost symbolical. Nevertheless their importance in drawing attention to the need and desirability of development plans must not be underrated even in such cases.

FIDES. It has been already pointed out that the funds provided by the French metropolitan government as outright grants have now reached 90 per cent of the estimated outlays under the plans. Their actual percentage has varied since the inception of the first plan in accordance with the local resources in each territory and with the type of project, the French experience being in this connection to some extent comparable with the British experience. It is therefore not easy to estimate overall percentages for the whole of the planned periods even in their case.

The Prosperity Fund and the Ten Year Plan Fund. The Surinam development plan has been firmly based on contributions by the Netherlands Government. The actual size and percentage of these contributions have varied at different stages and are now roughly of the order of one-third in outright grants and one-third in long-term loans guaranteed by the Netherlands Government, with the remaining third to be raised by the Surinam Government.

No grants have been made by the Belgian Government for development plans in its colonies.

[1] Cf. *Memorandum on Development in Sarawak*, 1947.
[2] Cf. The Gambia: *Report on Development and Welfare, 1950–2*, 1953, paras. 2, 16.

Loans. A second type of resources available for development purposes have been government loans, of local or of external origin. Indeed in the original plans loans seemed to loom large. In practice loans have so far turned out to be a less important source of revenue.

The funds raised through internal loans have been comparatively small. Some of these 'loans' have been simply transfers between funds, such as from the funds set up by the various public marketing boards to the development funds.

In the case of the British territories, the raising of general-purpose loans on the London market has not been very favourably looked upon by the Colonial Office or the United Kingdom Treasury. Uganda has been the most important exception in the early days of post-war development planning. Special circumstances, such as those in Kenya after the Mau Mau emergency, have of course softened the metropolitan attitude towards such loans. Better viewed have been the loans in connection with specific investment projects, such as those connected with mining, including private mining enterprises which have been allowed direct access to the metropolitan market. The resources of the IBRD have also been made available on a restricted scale for specific projects in connection with railway and hydro-electric power development.[1]

The French territories have had access to loans chiefly through the specially-set-up *Caisse Centrale* (CCFOM), which has not only advanced funds for private or public development projects but has even contributed much of the so-called local share of the development plans financed by FIDES.

The Belgian territories have raised loans both on the Belgian and on the Swiss markets as well as from international institutions, but it is only recently, with the speeding up of the implementation of the plan, that such loans are beginning to assume a greater importance. This is due in part to the gradual exhaustion of the reserves built up during the period of high prices for Congo's exports; but strong contributory factors are growing realization in the Congo that the capital development programme is making an essential contribution to economic development and that money invested in it is indeed economically productive; and the increasing confidence of the financial markets in the future of the territory.

---

[1] Cf. *Cmd 9375*, Table 1, for officially estimated Loan Funds for past plans, and *Cmd 9769*, Appendix III, for officially estimated Loan Funds for current plans. Unfortunately these estimates give no breakdown into local and foreign loans, nor into private and official sources for the loans.

Loans should become increasingly important throughout the colonial territories which have managed to prove to the outside world their economic viability and their financial trustworthiness, but so far planned development has made comparatively little use of borrowed funds.

Local Revenues. In the British and Belgian territories much of the development resources has been derived from local revenue raised mostly from royalties or other taxes on mineral production and exports, from export taxes on raw materials, and from import taxes, chiefly on consumption goods. Even in what seemed between 1946 and 1950 such hopeless cases as North Borneo and Sarawak the extraordinary (and unplanned) recovery in agricultural production, combined with the rapid increases in world prices, has resulted in a radical change of the situation, with local revenues becoming the main items of finance for development. Thus in North Borneo, with the exception of one advance early in 1950 of £100,000 from His Majesty's Treasury, it proved possible, both in 1950 and in 1951, to finance the reconstruction programme wholly from colony funds;[1] and in Sarawak it proved repeatedly necessary to revise the development programmes due to the rapid increase both in local revenues and in costs.

Planning Resources Arising from the Planned Development. Most of the colonial governments have been able to base part at least of their development plans fairly firmly on their knowledge of metropolitan funds allocations. The remaining part of their plans has tended to have less precise foundations. Some of their estimates have been based on their sometimes optimistic views on the possibility of raising loans—especially optimistic as far as the internal market was concerned, though on the whole the bulk of the loans envisaged were supposed to come from external sources. The remaining estimates have been based on their usually pessimistic projection of government revenues into the future. What the governments have refused on the whole to attempt or often even to envisage have been estimates of increased resources attributable to the development plans themselves. Except in the self-balancing departments, such as railway authorities or harbour authorities or electricity undertakings, departmental estimates can cover only the departmental recurrent costs of the capital development schemes and not their possible future contributions to the national income or to government revenue. The

[1] Cf. 'North Borneo Development Plans'. Introduction, in *Colombo Plan*, Part II (1951).

tendency has therefore been to envisage future resources on the basis of projected present resources minus projected present recurrent expenditure and minus additional recurrent expenditure arising from new capital development projects, thus leading to the rather paradoxical situation by which development implies a diminution of future budgetary resources available for additional development.

Thus the 1948 revision by the Development Commissioner, Sir Douglas Harris, of the Development Plan for Uganda based its new proposals on a revenue for 1957 somewhat less than that forecast for 1949 and only sufficient to enable the government of the day to meet the residual expenditure arising from the plan. In the words of Sir Douglas, 'to provide for more might well be stigmatized as rash; to provide for less as pusillanimous. A reasonably conservative view has much to commend it, since if revenues increase it is always easy to introduce some new services. It is much more difficult to curtail existing services if revenues fail to come up to expectations.'[1]

The position could be especially difficult when (as the Financial and Economic Adviser commented in the case of St Vincent, in the Windward Islands) there had been a concentration of (in that case CD & W) funds on the subsidization of recurrent services, because the necessity to meet residual charges on such schemes had to arise sooner or later and would continue to be increasingly reflected in the ordinary budget during the ensuing years.[2]

This preoccupation with future recurrent costs was strengthened in the British territories by words of warning from the Colonial Office concerning the undue weighting of plans on the side of welfare services or of very long-range economic developments whose contribution to future revenue was doubtful or long postponed but whose contribution to increased future costs was very real and unavoidable.

One instance only has been found in which the opposite case, of a possible diminution of recurrent costs following upon development expenditure, has also been put, though other territories may have had similar considerations in mind. In Kenya DARA stated that it realized that the early completion of certain development and reconstruction projects would reduce expenditure in the recurrent budget—housing for government servants being put forward as a case in point, as it would reduce the amount paid out in house allowances. As it also realized that certain projects might well enlarge the field from which

[1] Cf. Sir Douglas Harris, *The 1948 Revision of the Plan*, para. 9.
[2] Cf. St Vincent: *Memorandum on the Revision of the Development Plan*, by the Financial and Economic Adviser, Windward Islands, November 25, 1950.

taxation was drawn, both these points were to be borne in mind by the Authority in deciding priorities.[1]

In very few territories were even carefully optimistic views included in the earlier development plans concerning the possibility of increased resources following upon development projects. Thus in Tanganyika it was thought that while it would not be prudent to include in the Revised Plan more resources than could be 'reasonably foreseen' within the period up to 1956, the tempo of development in the territory was likely to speed up and with a more rapid economic progress the country should be quicker able to bear the recurrent burdens imposed by such expenditure and be in a position to undertake still further development and at a greater speed than that envisaged in the Revised Plan.[2]

In Northern Rhodesia some attempt was even made at a guess of a more precise nature concerning future growth, the planned residual expenditure arising from the plan being compared against an estimated figure for 1947 based on an 'annual rate of growth of 6 per cent (compound)' and computed from the approved 1951 estimates.[3]

Neither the Tanganyika nor the Northern Rhodesian references are very clear. It is not obvious whether Tanganyika assumed that the expected increase in economic activity would be a direct result of its development plans, nor is it quite clear whether the '6 per cent (compound)' in Northern Rhodesia in allowable increases in recurrent expenditure really implied an expectation of a similar increase in revenue, but some such views might have been held.

The IBRD Missions' Reports, which made definite attempts at assessing future increases both of national incomes and of government revenues arising from development plans,[4] have been, on the whole, a new departure in development planning in the colonial territories and are obviously closely connected with the much more highly centralized team approach of the IBRD, with the resulting investigation of the problems by sectors as opposed to administrative departments, and with the subsequent integration of the sectors into a general economic picture.

---

[1] Cf. DARA Report, 1947, para. 32.
[2] Cf. *Revised Development and Welfare Plan for Tanganyika, 1950–6*, 1951, chap. 2, para. 18.
[3] Cf. *Second (1951) Review of the Ten Year Development Plan of Northern Rhodesia*, 1951, section 2, para. 10.
[4] Cf. especially *The Economic Development of Nigeria*, pp. 686, 1953.

PRIORITIES

Within the limits of the forecast financial resources over the period of a plan arises what has been often held to be the most fundamental problem of planning, that of allocating priorities between the different sectors and schemes. To allocate priorities it is necessary to have a review both of needs and of the technical possibilities of using the estimated financial resources for the satisfaction of these needs.

The first attempts at planning in the British territories after the 1940 Act gave special emphasis to a catalogue of 'needs'. (This was in accordance with recommendations from the Colonial Office.) In quite a few colonies, especially in the West Indies and in the Far East, two sets of plans were drawn up as a result: they could be called a 'master plan', which included all desired development, and a 'practical plan', as in Granada;[1] or a 'long-term plan' and an 'immediate plan', as in 1950 in British Honduras, where the 'long-term plan' was defined also as a 'master plan'. The 'Departmental Sketch Plan' of 1945 in British Guiana, which was also a 'master plan', 'was virtually a schedule of social and economic *desiderata* without regard to the practical and financial possibilities of attainment'.[2] The object of the 1949 'Draft Development Plan' for the Federation of Malaya was twofold: to express the social and economic purposes which should form the 'target of endeavour' for the people of Malaya, and to present an agreed six-year programme of development which would be 'at once well balanced and within practical financial limits'. Throughout the plan these two aspects were treated separately and referred to as 'long-term Objectives' and 'Draft Programme, 1950–5'.[3]

Obviously even in the most realistic of plans there must be a fringe of projects whose implementation will have to depend upon future financial resources which, as we have seen, could only be forecast within fairly wide limits. When the device of using two plans was eschewed two methods of dealing with this fringe were used.

The first method was that, recommended in *Cmd 6713*, Memorandum, paragraph 1c, and used especially in some of the West Indian territories, of bunching projects by groups in accordance with group priorities.

[1] Cf. *A Plan for the Development of the Colony of Granada, 1946–56*.
[2] Cf. British Guiana, Papers relating to Development Planning: *Legislative Council Paper No. 8/9*, 1947, para. 7.
[3] Cf. *The 1949 Draft Development Plan for the Federation of Malaya*, p. 1.

Thus in Barbados the projects were divided into categories as follows:

(i) schemes to which the Government was already committed, such as CD & W scheme D217;
(ii) essential and urgent;
(iii) essential but not urgent;
(iv) highly desirable;
(v) desirable.

In Jamaica the schemes were divided into three priorities. Under the Jamaican system even projects which, on the basis of the estimated financial possibilities, were most unlikely to be undertaken could be included in the plan.

The second method was to make one single plan, and to review it at frequent intervals in the light of changing financial resources and of costs. It would then be left to some extent to each department to put forward new claims in case of increasing resources, or to readjust its expenditure between projects in the case of increasing costs, obviously in accordance with the usual control and accountancy rulings.

Reconstruction and Development. The pre-1945 plans were quickly superseded by the new needs and possibilities arising with the end of the war. The first realistic attempts at planning in the sense that an implementation of the plans could be foreseen and provided for occurred even in the British territories only with the end of hostilities. The immediate problem in many territories, and especially in those which had been under enemy occupation as in the Far East, or near the battle front as in East Africa, was to try and repair wartime damage and neglect. In the first post-war development plans, therefore, reconstruction obviously was given high priority. The North Borneo Plan, for example, was actually called a 'Reconstruction and Development Plan', and Kenya set up a Development and Reconstruction Authority.

But shortages had developed throughout the colonies, from the serious understaffing of the administrative services to the general wear and tear which had not been made good throughout the war, such as, for example, in the case of the railways, where both the rolling-stock and the understructure were in great need of repair and replacement. It seemed obvious that such unspent financial reserves as had been built up in certain territories during the war should be earmarked first of all for making good such wartime deficiencies.

The plans thus tended to contain two types of projects, even though seldom separated along these lines, namely those which would bring the territories back to their pre-war standards, and those which would enable them to move ahead beyond such standards. But as deficiencies as well as wear and tear were widespread by the end of the war, the desire to put them right in fact meant that, within a series of projects in each sector or department, the repair and maintenance projects would tend to have some automatic priority over 'development' projects. Possibly among the most interesting, from an accountancy point of view, is the attempt to bring establishments up to strength. There does not seem to be any case where an increase in staffing has been considered 'development', if such increase had occurred within the establishment strength.

The problem of priorities in development is thus a problem which has tended to become especially important after the return to 'normalcy'. The main influences at work in decisions on such priorities seem to have been, on the one hand, advice or directives from the metropolitan governments, and on the other the local views on local needs.

CHAPTER 13

The Metropolitan Governments and the Problem of Priority Allocation

ADVICE FROM THE METROPOLITAN GOVERNMENT: BRITAIN

Economic Viability and the Standard of Living. In the case of the British territories the advice from the Colonial Office has tended to vary round a central theme. This central theme, in accordance with well-established views, has been that the colonial territories must aim ultimately at economic viability, that they should be able to stand on their own feet, that, as the Secretary of State for the Colonies mentioned in his Statement of Policy,[1] 'a colony should have only those services which it can afford to maintain out of its own resources'. The variations on this theme have been concerned with the length of time before such viability ought to be reached and, intimately connected with this, with the standard of living to be aimed at immediately and at various stages on the path to such viability.

An additional problem in certain cases, especially in that of the West Indies but also in East and Central Africa and in the Far East, has been the size of the unit for which such viability could best be reached.

In the case of the West Indies the Royal Commission had suggested twenty years as the period during which United Kingdom grants would be necessary for ensuring the necessary social and economic developments to set the territories on their feet.[2] This period of twenty years seems to have been suggested more as a nice long period than to have been reached by some intricate calculations. In certain ways it might be said that what the Royal Commission really meant was that only a concerted effort over a very long period of time could hope to solve the problems of the West Indies, and twenty years

[1] Cf. *Cmd 6175*, para. 6.
[2] Cf. *Cmd 6607*.

would be none too long for that. The Colonial Office not only accepted this view for the West Indies but widened it to include all other colonial territories.

But, of course, a territory could—in a sense—stand on its own feet at any time. The discontinuation of an external grant would bring about a lowering of the standard of living, but standards of living are relative concepts. It might increase the incidence of disease and of mortality, intensify social strains and lower the educational standards, but these again are all relative quantities. What the Royal Commission had therefore done, in fact, was to establish certain standards it considered essential, to recommend the external funds it thought necessary to ensure the attainment of these standards, and to guess at the minimum period of time within which the economies of the West Indian territories would have developed sufficiently to enable such standards to be maintained without any further outside help.

The Colonial Office and His Majesty's Government in the United Kingdom were faced with a similar problem in the rest of the colonial empire: they had to decide what standards of living should be aimed at in the various territories at various future stages, and at what date it would be possible for such standards of living to be maintained entirely from local resources. As their views on these matters varied, so did their advice to local administrations and their emphasis on welfare versus economic development in their public pronouncements. In 1940, under the influence of the *West India Royal Commission's Report*, as well as in reaction to the 'economic' spirit of the 1929 Colonial Development Act, the emphasis tended to be on welfare. Thus, though in his Statement of Policy the Secretary of State, Mr MacDonald, had said that:

'The first emphasis in this much enlarged policy of colonial development will be on the improvement of the economic position of the colonies. That is the primary requirement, upon which advance in other directions is largely consequential. It is by economic development that the colonies will be placed in a position to devote their resources, to the maximum extent possible, to the provision of those government and other services which the interests of their people demand. Assistance from United Kingdom funds should be effectively related to what the colonies can do for themselves . . .'[1]

[1] Cf. *Cmd 6175*, para. 11.

he qualified these statements during the debate on the Second Reading of the CD & W Bill, as follows:

'Our object under this legislation is to develop the colonies so that as far as possible they become self-supporting units. But in the meantime their citizens must enjoy a proper standard of social services, and we shall count as qualifying for assistance under this Bill every part of the health and medical activities and every part of the educational activities of a colonial government. In this legislation the word "development" has not a narrow materialistic interpretation. It certainly covers the development of the material, economic, resources of a territory, but it also covers everything which ministers to the physical, mental or moral development of the colonial peoples of whom we are the trustees. ... If this Bill goes through Parliament we shall be able in future to contribute towards not only the initial costs of establishment but the running costs of any of those services which are needed in these days for the proper welfare of colonial peoples.'[1]

The realities of war enforced a drastic cutting down on development expenditure on the basis of an entirely different set of priorities, that of the war emergency, leading to an emphasis on the kinds of projects which could be undertaken without recourse to resources needed for the war itself. But with the end of the war in sight, the Colonial Office could return once more to the problem of development priorities in terms of the needs of the colonial territories.

During the end of the war period both Oliver Stanley, who as Conservative Secretary of State for the Colonies in the National Union Government moved the 1945 CD & W Bill, and Mr Hall, who as Labour Secretary of State a few months later was entrusted with its implementation, tried to keep a fair balance of emphasis between economic development and welfare.

Thus Colonel Stanley, during the debate on the second reading of the Colonial Development and Welfare Bill, 1945, said:

'In the long run the social standards of a country must depend upon its own resources, must depend upon the skill and energy of its own people and the wise and full use which they make of their internal wealth.... The object is to give the territories the help they want and must have if they are to start for themselves the process of developing their own resources ... it is to be in the nature of a

[1] Cf. *Hansard*, May 21, 1940, cols. 47–8.

THE PROBLEM OF PRIORITY ALLOCATION 141

pump primer to enable people to start their education and health services, to develop their communications and to deal with their water power in the confident belief that when they have been enabled to make that start it will lead to an increase in their own resources, and that out of their resources they will then be able to maintain a decent social standard.'[1]

And Mr Hall, in his *Circular Despatch* of November 12, 1945, stated:

'There are great possibilities in the years that lie ahead for raising the standards of health, education, social welfare and general well-being of colonial peoples if these expanded services are based upon improved economic efficiency and increased production. The primary requisite still is an improvement of the economic position in the colonial dependencies, the utilization of their natural resources to the greatest extent possible, and the widening of opportunity for human endeavour and enterprise.'[2]

Nevertheless, the mood of Britain in 1945 was towards an expansion of the social services, and this seems to have communicated itself to some at least of the colonial territories' officials. If any change in the balance between economic and welfare projects had to be requested by the Colonial Office in the development plans of the colonial territories which were being sent in, it was towards a greater emphasis on economic development than was being envisaged in some of the colonies.

Thus, in the case of Zanzibar, the Secretary of State had to point out that the development programme was heavily weighted on the side of the social services, the majority of the available funds being allocated to education, health, and town improvements, and definitely not towards economic development as usually understood. He specially emphasized that though he considered the agricultural part of the programme to be 'well conceived and sound' he could not regard it as representing the last word on economic development in Zanzibar, which depended too much on the clove industry. If its development was to be sustained over a long period it was essential that no opportunity of increasing its basic resources should be lost.[3]

[1] *Hansard*, February 7, 1945, col. 2098.
[2] *Cmd 6713*, para. 3.
[3] Cf. *Programme of Social and Economic Development in the Zanzibar Protectorate, for the Ten Year Period 1946–55*, 1946. Appendix: 'Statement of Views Communicated by the Secretary of State in the Ten Year Development Programme prepared in Zanzibar,' p. 32, para. 11.

In Tanganyika the Secretary of State informed the Governor that he thought that a disproportionate share of the total cost of the 1944 programme had been allocated to social services, public works and buildings, township development, etc., and an insufficient sum to economic development. He pointed out that the extent to which the territory could afford the proposed expansion of the social and other services described in the memorandum would depend very largely on the extent to which the 'economic resources (and—by implication—the taxable capacity of the inhabitants) of the territory were expanded'. It was consequently desirable that the expenditure to be undertaken in the immediate future should be weighted on the side of economic development.[1]

This, of course, does not mean that the Colonial Office approach was not itself too much inclined towards welfare: it would not be easy to make a judgement today on what the right balance ought to have been. It means only that some of the colonial administrations were even more desirous of developing welfare activities than the Colonial Office itself.

There is no doubt, though, that the Colonial Office has been steadily moving towards a greater emphasis on economic development. Its 1945 position in post-war planning could today be called a maximum welfare position. It has been shown[2] that the Gambia *Memorandum on Development* of 1946 had already stated that correspondence subsequent to March 1946 had indicated that the assumption that in the special circumstances of the Gambia a programme of development should be weighted on the side of social rather than economic development was no longer considered valid by His Majesty's Government in the United Kingdom.

The 1947 financial crisis in the United Kingdom seems to have provoked a moment of panic throughout the colonial empire, even though the financial circumstances in the colonies themselves were on the whole little affected by the United Kingdom difficulties except in so far as the raising of loans on the London Market was concerned, at that time a matter of minor importance. This had strong effects along the lines, already followed by the Colonial Office, of a movement away from the social services and towards the development of productive activities. It certainly enabled the Colonial Office to impress this policy more forcefully on the territories asking for its views and advice.

[1] Cf. *A Ten Year Development and Welfare Plan for Tanganyika Territory*, 1946.
[2] Cf. The Gambia: *Memorandum on Development*, 1946, para. 2.

Views on Individual Priorities. Though concerned with what it happened to consider at various times the proper balance between welfare and production as applied to individual colonies, the Colonial Office seems to have had few general views on individual priorities. The exceptions have not, on the whole, been very happy.

In 1940 Mr MacDonald told the House of Commons that he strongly supported the view that one of the modifications needed in colonial agriculture was a movement towards the establishment of subsistence agriculture. He thought it wrong that a great many native producers should be engaged in producing commodities for export and not in producing the foodstuffs which they themselves required for consumption. One of the lines of advance, not only in the case of the African colonies but in the case also of the West Indies and other colonies, should therefore be a modification of the policy of spending too much effort on export crops in the direction of more and more on subsistence agriculture. That, he added, was the deliberate policy of the Colonial Office at the time and he was certain that the local governments in drawing up their plans would place a good deal of emphasis on the desirability of that policy.[1]

That deliberate policy by the Colonial Office towards subsistence agriculture may have been influenced by the report of the Royal Commission on the West Indies which recommended the curtailment of special single export crops in favour of mixed farming on a smallholding basis. The Evans Commission's comments eight years later on the effects of that policy were not favourable. The Evans Commission pointed out that in the highly industrialized countries of Europe, where there is profit in such individual mixed farming on a small scale from that of allotment holder up to the mixed farm of, say, 100 acres, the consumer is never far away and a highly organized system of markets exists. A wholly agrarian community, on the other hand, such as that in existence in the colonies, could not live by 'taking in each other's washing' and must look to bulk exports to pay for the necessary imports.[2] Though the Evans Commission report implied that the Moyne Commission's recommendations may have been valid in the circumstances of its time, it could only condemn their effects, among which it mentioned the 'defects and lack of purpose in the Agricultural Departments' which had to be attributed

[1] Cf. *Hansard*, May 21, 1940, col. 119.
[2] Cf. *Cmd 7533, Report of the British Guiana and British Honduras Settlement Commission*, September 1948, para. 8 (i).

to the 'somewhat sweeping, and in our view unfortunate, condemnation by the Royal Commission of commercial agriculture and its advocacy of smallholding mixed farming'. The immediate effects in British Honduras of the Moyne recommendations had been the maintenance of 'stagnant agricultural stations' and the diversion of the staff to 'somewhat uninformed instruction' of smallholders.[1]

This concentration on self-sufficiency, on holding the line, though a natural reaction to the blizzard which had hit export agriculture throughout the world during the great depression and strengthened by the unpleasant tendency to high fluctuations in the prices of colonial export products, was continued in the changed circumstances of the post-war world as a matter of official policy. As late as 1950 the East Africa High Commission, with the obvious blessing of the Colonial Office, was attempting to work out long-range plans for 'such economic self-sufficiency in East Africa as examination in detail may show to be practical'. It was hoped that 'the protection from dumping and sudden external price collapse' which such a policy would give to agricultural products, and the encouragement it would provide to local production, could do much to put agriculture 'on a sound footing' and to create the confidence required to give a further stimulus to expansion and development.[2]

A similar defensive approach has also been shown by the Colonial Office on the question of foreign investment in the colonies. Even the Conservative Oliver Stanley, while affirming in the House of Commons his belief in 'a growing opportunity for private investment, from capital outside the territories', continued by stating that as it was obviously desirable that the people themselves should be linked, through their capital contributions, with the industries of their own country, it was necessary to guard against the danger that 'all the holes will be filled up, that all industrial opportunities will be taken' and that when people became more investment-minded and more managerially fit they would find no place left for them.[3] This ingrained belief in the basically stagnant character of the countries' economies, which seems to have been common to the Colonial Office in London and to its officials throughout the colonies, showed itself especially strongly in the widespread policy against allowing further outside commercial interests to enter the territories, on the assumption that the trading total is fixed, and a greater

[1] Cf. *op. cit.* paras. 6, 21 (i).
[2] Cf. *Report of the Planning Committee*, Kenya, 1951, para. 39.
[3] Cf. *Hansard*, February 7, 1945, col. 2100.

share to outsiders can only imply a smaller share for the local inhabitants.[1]

The departures from the position of self-sufficiency which seem to have been favourably looked upon by the Colonial Office at various times have been connected with large-scale, preferably mechanized, agricultural schemes; with diversification of crops; with industrial development, especially through officially sponsored industrial development corporations. A number of experts, or of expert commissions, have been sent out from London to investigate and advise on possibilities of mechanized development and large-scale agriculture in East Africa, West Africa and the Caribbean; a number of studies on various crops and their suitability for different territories has been published; and, though less has been done from London on problems of industrialization, the question seems to have been kept at least under constant review.

On the social services side little guidance on priorities as between the different sectors, especially concerning their possible influence on economic development, seems to have been given from London, though a fair amount of detailed advice on methods and organization within each service has always been available.

DECISIONS BY THE METROPOLITAN GOVERNMENT: FRANCE

The mainly advisory approach of the British metropolitan government to colonial planning is not, of course, the only possible one. In the case of the French development plans for the colonial territories the influence on priorities of the central planning authorities has been much more direct and definite, both due to the metropolitan character of the planning committees and to the fact that most of the investment funds have been metropolitan funds.

The first plan, drawn up in 1947 in Paris, gave detailed estimates for a planned total public investment between 1947 and 1956 of some 190,000,000,000 metropolitan francs, divided into two five-year 'slices' of some 103,000,000,000 and some 87,000,000,000 respectively.[2] In the first quinquennium some 47·5 per cent was allocated to transport and communications, some 23 per cent to production and

[1] Cf. *East Africa Royal Commission Report, 1953–5, Cmd 9475*; also P. T. Bauer, *West African Trade, 1955*, and Bauer and Yamey, Economic Aspects of Immigration Policy in Nigeria and Gold Coast, *South African Journal of Economics*, June 1954, pp. 223 ff.
[2] Cf. *Premier rapport de la commission de modernisation des territoires d'outremer*, Janvier 1948; especially *Tableau II*. The percentages have been computed by the author.

some 26 per cent to social services. The second quinquennium had about the same proportions of funds allocated to transport and communications, but the proportion of investments in the productive sector were going to diminish slightly to just over 21 per cent, while those in the social services were going to increase to almost 28 per cent.

The proportions for the whole decennium were thus of some 47·5 per cent for transport and communications, a little over 22 per cent for production (of which agriculture, livestock and forestry almost 16 per cent, electricity almost 5 per cent, mines just over 1 per cent, and a negligible amount for 'miscellaneous' activities) and a little over 27 per cent for the social services. The remaining 3 per cent were allocated to central activities of research and mapping. If the 17,000,000,000 francs of central funds to be spent on the imperial air network and the 6,600,000,000 to be spent on the inter-colonial telecommunication service were to be added—though it is not easy to apportion them between the various parts of the French Union—the proportion to be spent over the decennium on transport and communications would be raised to well over 50 per cent of the total.

The plan indicated also the total amount of private investments expected by the planners during the two quinquennia by sectors. Such 'expectations' were, in fact, little more than guesses and turned out to be unduly optimistic.

What is especially interesting in the general approach of the first plan—besides the fact of its detailed decisions by the metropolitan government—is the expected diminution of investments both in the public and in the private sectors during the second quinquennium. In the public sector the planned expenditure was some 18 per cent higher in the first quinquennium than in the second, and in the private sector it was as much as 21 per cent higher, some 52,000,000,000 as compared to some 43,000,000,000 francs. The plan was, in fact, conceived of as much as a reconstruction plan as a development plan, and once the wartime deficiencies had been made good investments were supposed to begin to tail off.

Actual investments between 1946 and 1953 amounted to 336,000,000,000 francs for the overseas territories and departments, of which 49 per cent were for transport and communications, 12 per cent for agricultural and livestock production, 11 per cent for electricity, 15 per cent for the social services and 6 per cent for research, including agriculture, forestry and mining.[1]

[1] Cf. *Financement des plans de développement économique et social des territoires français d'outre-mer* (no date), dealing with the period 1946–53. CCFOM, internal paper.

THE PROBLEM OF PRIORITY ALLOCATION 147

This over-emphasis on transport and communications, and on non-productive or not immediately productive sectors generally, was severely criticized by an increasing number of both experts and officials, including the planning committees of 1953–4. The emphasis had been based, according to an internal summary,[1] on the view that the modernization and the extension of ports, railways and roads was going to contribute effectively to the development of agricultural production and create conditions favourable to the industrial development of the territories. But, as the summary pointed out, production had not grown at the same speed as investments. The recurrent costs of the new installations as well as the repayments of the loans threatened to lead to unduly heavy tax burdens for the territories if there was not a proportional increase in their resources to match this increase in costs.

FIDES investments, which included all the outright grants to the overseas territories, had been, between 1946 and 1953, 63·5 per cent for communications, 15 per cent for the development of rural economy and 21 per cent for social services. By the time the 'transitional year', 1954–5, had been reached the proportions had changed fairly radically, as a result of the above-mentioned criticisms, to 41 per cent for communications, 35·3 per cent for economic development, with the social services remaining more or less steady at 21·6 per cent.[2]

The full 1954–8[3] four-year plan envisaged a total expenditure of 372,700,000,000 francs from metropolitan funds, of which 348,000,000,000 on the overseas territories and 24,700,000,000 on the overseas departments. The spending was planned on an increasing scale over the first three years, with the fourth-year spending in theory the same as that for the third year. In fact, taking into account the usual delays due to the various kinds of planning difficulties and of the shortages of supplies to which plans seem to be prone, year by year increases in actual spending could be expected throughout the four years.[4]

Both the increase in total spending, larger in the four years 1954–8

[1] Cf. *Financement des programmes de développement économique et social dans les territoires et départments d'outre-mer en 1954*, May 24, 1955. CCFOM, internal paper.
[2] Cf. *op. cit.*
[3] The exact dates for the plan are difficult to fix, though there is a growing tendency to place it between July 7, 1953, and June 30, 1957, to fit in with FIDES budgeting.
[4] Cf. *Le financement des programmes de développement économique et social des territoires et départments d'outre-mer en 1955*, June 4, 1956. CCFOM, internal paper.

than in the whole of the previous seven years, and the increasing rate of spending during these four years thus show a departure from the former tailing-off approach at least as interesting as the increase in the emphasis on agricultural production as compared to transport (with social services stationary) already indicated in the transitional year 1954–5.

On the whole, the last four-year plans for the individual territories within the French colonial empire may be said to conform to some rough 45:35:20 proportion, for transport, production and social services respectively, though there are appreciable variations around these proportions from territory to territory, in accordance with local problems and circumstances. Though this seems to have been nowhere stated in so many words, this rough 45:35:20 proportion may be taken to represent an indication of what the central planning authorities felt were the right proportions for the 1954–8 plans, and it is the proportions which the local planning authorities, whose importance in the field of planning has been steadily increasing since 1946, seem to have been taking as some kind of general guide.

CHAPTER 14

The Territorial Governments and the Problem of Priority Allocation

THE ADMINISTRATIVE UNITS

IT has already been pointed out that the colonial territories, with the exception of a few geographical units such as certain fairly isolated islands, tend to be administrative entities set up artificially as a result of historical accidents. No doubt this applies not only to the colonies: it could be said that most present-day countries throughout the world are artificially delimited due to historical accidents. But in the case of many such countries there has been sufficient time over the generations for them to develop a number of features making for an organic integration of their originally rather dissimilar parts. In the case of most of the colonies time has been short. Development plans within most colonial territories have therefore had to face this problem of administrative units which did not necessarily coincide with the 'natural units'. Some of these administrative units have been larger than the 'natural' units; some, for example in the West Indies, have been much smaller.

The planning bodies have usually been emanations of the territorial administrations and their planning units have therefore been the administrative units. If the central territorial administration was doubled by some kind of regional, 'federal' administrations, as in Nigeria or in the French African Federations, then regional plans have sometimes also been put forward, themselves normally based on artificial sub-territorial delimitations. The principle of planning for an 'administrative' unit has not been appreciably changed by such 'regional' planning.

With a good deal of straining at the truth it might be said that the immediate concern of planning has been the development of administrative activities and only at one remove that of the territory itself, even though the development of the territory may have been the ultimate aim.

With the administrative unit as the whole for which planning must be undertaken, the planning problems have tended to be seen in terms of the administration's problems as they have arisen over a number of years. A decision to plan does not change any of the basic facts within the administrative unit to be planned, such as its geography, its climate, the quality and the distribution of its population. The rapidity with which many of the plans have been drawn up indicates that all that was needed in many cases was simply to pull out of the respective files projects which had already been discussed and studied in the past.

Thus in Tanganyika 'the committee proceeded to select from the wealth of material at its disposal such schemes as were considered to be best suited for early implementation',[1] and in Kenya it was considered sufficient to give the departments only three months[2] to prepare and submit five-year development plans. It would be difficult, as already indicated, to point out in the Gold Coast major development projects included in the post Second World War plans which had not already been at least mentioned and often exhaustively discussed in the plans put forward some thirty years earlier by Governor Guggisberg.

In the case of the British territories the submission of projects for financial allocations under the 1940 CD & W Act had furthermore implied a review at that time by each territory of its needs and possibilities, reviews which could only have been of help when an overall plan had to be drawn up in the post-war period.

THE 'COMMON SENSE' VERSUS THE 'SCIENTIFIC' APPROACH

There seem to have been two main approaches to the problem of determining priorities. The first approach could be called the common-sense approach, or maybe the instinctive approach. Firmly based on the past experience and activities of individual departments and of heads of departments, as well as on the relative share of departments in the total resources of the Government, it proceeds to deal from case to case with possibilities of expansion having due regard to the available resources. Thus decision on a new road between A and B would be taken because it is well known by the respective department as well as by all the people having to travel between A and B that a new road is needed; and past experience, as well as guesses at possible future traffic expansion, would determine

[1] Cf. *An Outline of Post-war Development Proposals*, 1944, para. 5.
[2] Cf. *Circular Letter No. 44* of April 20, 1944.

THE PROBLEM OF PRIORITY ALLOCATION 151

the technical standards to which the road is to be built. The general ceiling on the building of roads would be settled by similar needs for expansion of other departments, such as education, agriculture, health, etc., needs whose relative importance would also be determined by past experience and general reasonableness within the administration.

As far as these relative shares between departments are concerned we have already seen that in the British territories there has been some disagreement in certain cases with the Colonial Office experts, who, looking at the matter from a greater distance from every-day problems and preoccupations than the territorial administration, have felt that the local planners had allocated too large a share to the social services. In such disagreements the Colonial Office has normally had the upper hand through its control of CD & W funds and the necessary readjustments have been made by the local authorities.

The second approach to the problem of determining priorities is much more ambitious. It involves an attempt at a completely new rethinking of the whole problem of the development of the territory concerned, without regard to the existing activities of the administrative departments, though obviously their knowledge and experience is taken into account. The results of this second approach, especially when undertaken by the administration itself and not by outside experts, have not necessarily been very different from those reached in territories which had been using the first approach. This might indicate either that piece-meal development has been able to keep fairly close to the needs and possibilities of the territories concerned or else that the process of rethinking has been too much influenced, even if involuntarily, by the previous administrative experience.

It is practically impossible to subject the first, 'common-sense', approach to a detailed critical analysis as it is made up of a very large number of individual schemes supplementing or expanding existing activities, and the overall results, as well as their justification, tend to be purely statistical. The general conception behind the plan, when there is one, is of the rule-of-thumb variety. Its advantage may well be a greater flexibility and easier adjustment of each scheme and project to changing circumstances even though there may be less conscious direction towards this or that major objective. The second, rethinking approach provides a more fruitful field for analysis.

Pet Projects versus General Expansion. The main change introduced by the 1940 and the 1945 CD & W Acts and by the ten-year development proposals in the French, Belgian, Dutch and British territories was the certainty for each territory that definite funds would be available for undertaking development projects. The temptation, induced by this sudden availability of funds, to pull out of pigeon-holes pet projects which had been continuously postponed was no doubt very great, both because of the emotional significance of many such projects, and because they provided a simple, ready and neat answer to the metropolitan demands for development proposals. Thus in the Gambia the re-siting of the capital from Bathurst to Kombo St Mary seems to have been the pivot for most of the early development planning, though it had to be finally abandoned. The Bridgetown deep-water harbour in Barbados which 'overshadows all other developments and must be given first priority',[1] the Northern Territories Railway and the Volta River Project in the Gold Coast, the Central African Railway Link, as well as a host of smaller projects within each department, which seemed at last to have some chance of implementation, were put forward either as individual schemes or as ' part' of the plan.

The number of such pet projects has undoubtedly been large, but their importance within individual plans has varied according to local circumstances. On the whole, the smaller and poorer the territory, the greater the share of the pet projects—though some exceptions, as in the case of the Gold Coast, can be quoted—and the reason seems rather obvious: even one simple and fairly small project may loom large in St Kitts and Nevis.

But development planning has tended on the whole to include increasingly large amounts for the expansion of existing activities as opposed to isolated projects. Sometimes, of course, it is not easy to differentiate between the two: are university colleges an expansion of educational activities or separate projects? Are a new harbour, a new and costly bridge, an expansion of existing transport facilities or separate projects?

The distinction might have to be made on the basis of a number of considerations, such as the individual share in the total planned outlays, the changes in standards introduced by the new project, its effects on the community, its power to concentrate the community's attention on itself as an individual project and not only as one of a series of the same type. At least psychologically the distinction is nevertheless interesting and can be important.

Priorities have had to be determined with both kinds of projects in mind: those involving an expansion of existing activities, and

[1] Cf. Barbados: *Development Finance, 1955–60*, para. 6.

those having in some way a separate identity. It is, on the whole, in the expansion of existing activities that priority decisions have presented the greatest problems to the planning organizations. The single separate type of project is usually almost by definition indivisible. The decision to be reached is therefore simply on whether the project should or should not be undertaken. An expansion of existing activities, on the other hand, involves in addition the need for decisions on the ultimate scale of expansion and on the rate of expansion to reach that scale. Expansions automatically involve the difficult problem of phasing.

The Problems of Capital Investment and of Recurrent Cost Planning.
Another interesting dichotomy in development plans is that between the public works or capital-investment plans on the one hand and the long-term overall budgets on the other. As we have seen in the section dealing with the administrative machinery, these two types have been evolved over the last few years because of the need to deal with certain problems, chief among which have been those of providing for the increased recurrent costs resulting from development expenditure and of fitting development into the changing patterns of public control following especially on the increased participation by non-officials in decision making.

In the British territories the CD & W Acts provided for the inclusion in schemes eligible for grants from the CD & W Fund of some of the recurrent costs for at least a limited period. As a result development plans in the various territories at first tended to cover both once-for-all outlays and some of the recurrent expenditure arising from such outlays. Development budgeting thus led to the introduction alongside the normal, annual budget, which included established recurrent costs, of a long-term budget whose instalments were often also approved annually, but which included the new capital investments plus the recurrent costs attributable to previous investments under the development plan.

Such recurrent costs have tended to increase with the passage of years and the addition of new development projects. A stage was thus reached in many territories when so-called development planning resulted, from the accountancy point of view, in budgeting for two different types of *recurrent* costs, with capital investments included as practically only an appendix to one of these two recurrent-costs budgets. This did not seem the best solution to the problem of plan-making.

One way out has been to prune all recurrent expenditure from the long-term plans, transforming such plans into capital investment plans.

Northern Rhodesia decided in 1951 to transfer 'recurrent development expenditure' from the plan to the departmental heads, transforming the plan into a public-works plan.[1] Similarly Trinidad, which has had a fairly long experience of programming development works, the first such plan having been approved in 1938, emphasized in its 1950 memorandum on the 1950–5 economic programme that the memorandum contained details of major public capital investments required in Trinidad and Tobago, together with proposals for the execution of part of the programme over a period of five years. It recognized that fiscal policies, the development of industries, and other matters of importance for economic development, and which 'the government of the colony has in hand', were not included in the memorandum except as incidental to certain capital investments, but it justified this by pointing out that the programme of public capital investment had a special significance as the foundation of the colony's economic development.[2]

In Kenya the changes were more gradual and at first accidental. Though the first plan dealt with both capital investments and recurrent costs, for purposes of implementation of the plan a special organization, DARA, had been set up as from August 1, 1945, to deal only with capital investments, recurrent costs being taken care of in the normal annual budget, and the Authority had its own fund and budget established as from January 1, 1946. Though this did not, at the time, arise from theoretical considerations relating to a double budget system but simply from the decision to charge DARA with executive responsibility for the ten-year plan, later on various steps were taken to draw 'a logical distinction' between capital and recurrent transactions.[3]

'Purely' capital investment programmes do not, of course, necessarily mean what they seem to imply. There are certain facts of life which must be taken into consideration, such as the ingenuity of individual administrators in squeezing out additional funds for their departments. Recurrent transport costs, for example, can be very easily transformed into the capital investment item of a purchase of vehicles. It is unofficially accepted that up to 20 per cent of the capital investment grants made by FIDES may in fact be for such

---

[1] Cf. *Second (1951) Review of the Ten Year Development Plan.*
[2] Cf. *Trinidad and Tobago Five Year Economic Programme,* 1950, vol. i, Introduction, p. 1.
[3] Cf. Kenya: *Sessional Paper No. 51,* 1955, para. 97.

camouflaged purposes, and this though FIDES has grown highly expert at detecting and rejecting such items.

The other solution to the problem of development budgeting has been to transform the annual budgets into planning budgets by extending the normal yearly budget estimating and accounting to cover a number of years.

Uganda was among the first to adopt this device and possibly the most radical in its attempt. The 1948 revision of the development plan covered expenditure of every kind, whether required for the maintenance of existing services or for the initiation of new ones. It thus provided a complete financial plan covering the following eight years.[1] Nigeria, under the influence of the plan of the IBRD Mission, drew up a development plan for 1955–60 which it called an 'economic programme'. The justification for the wide contents of the plan was the impossibility of drawing up a programme for the 'development' services, i.e. the services dealing with social questions or with projects of direct economic significance, without at the same time taking into account in one way or another the demands of services whose economic significance is less obvious, like security, defence and administration, as well as all the resources which are likely to be available.[2]

That these alternatives are not final may be shown by the reversion of Uganda, after a rather planless interval due to unforeseen changes of income and resources, to a purely capital development programme in 1954,[3] while Kenya, on the other hand, decided to integrate its capital development expenditure into its normal budgetary arrangements under a 'below the line' system.[4]

This uncertainty as to what the plan should include may well be inherent in the present approach to planning. In any case, it seems to have been a widespread feature of the plans in the territories under discussion.

Treatment of Cross-effects as Negligible. If there has often been uncertainty as to what a plan should include, there seems at first sight to have been more agreement on what a plan should aim at. The stated purpose of most plans could be summarized as (*a*) an increase in the productive potentialities of the territory, to (*b*) enable higher standards of living.

[1] Cf. 1948 *Revision of the Development Plan for Uganda*, para. 6.
[2] Cf. *The Economic Programme of the Government of the Federation of Nigeria, 1955–60*, para. 4.
[3] Cf. *A Five Year Capital Development Plan, 1955–60*.
[4] Cf. Kenya: *Sessional Paper No. 51, 1955*.

Though it could be argued, as in fact it has been done in some of the plans, that the two objectives of increased productivity and of higher standards of living are logically connected, the tendency has been to treat them separately, in fact if not always in theory. From the point of view of the 'plan', as well as from that of administrative action, the direct influence of increased productive investment on welfare and even more so of increased welfare on output have both tended to be treated as quantities of the second order of smallness and therefore neglected. This has greatly facilitated the choice of priorities between social and economic investment.

In the territories where the administration was 'welfare' conscious, social investment has tended to depend on the often rather optimistic views of the administration on 'what can be afforded' or, if articulate local groups existed, on some compromise between the views of the administration and the usually even more optimistic local opinions, and economic investment has been allocated the remaining resources. This seems to have applied especially to British territories.

The opposite process has occurred in the other territories, though for varying reasons. In the French territories it has been the comparative aloofness of the *Comité Directeur* of FIDES in Paris and of its immediate organs which has enabled a concentration on economic development, social development having to be content with the remainder term. In the Belgian territories the unchallenged authority of a professional administration has had the same result. In Surinam the careful analysis by experts and expert teams from three different sources, Surinam itself, the Netherlands and the International Bank, has made it possible to convince the population as well as the political leaders that improvements in the social sector could only follow upon higher productivity. In the British territories, when economic development has succeeded in pushing social investments into second place it is usually possible to discover that causes similar to those indicated for the other territories have been at work.

Some kind of a circular reasoning is, of course, implied in this share-out, as 'what can be afforded' for social development depends to some extent on the planners' views on what is urgently necessary in the economic field, and vice versa.

A second simplification has further facilitated decisions on priorities within the plan: effects of developments within one certain limited sector on the future needs or potentialities within that same sector have generally, and with the exception of recurrent costs, not been taken into account. This has applied both to the social services sectors and to the economic sectors. Thus a planned increase in primary education did not affect the plans for an increase in secondary education: each was planned on its own merits. Of course, if one increase depended upon another—if expansion of primary education depended upon more teachers and thus on an expansion of teacher training colleges—attempts would normally have been made to take this into account, though instances could be found where even this has been overlooked. What has not generally been allowed for has been an increase in the demand for a certain service, such as better river-crossing arrangements, due to a previous increase in the supply of a connected service within the same sector, such as better roads in the district; or an increase in resources due to a previous investment.

Human Resources and Natural Resources. Within this simplified scheme certain patterns seem to become defined. In the case of economic development one pattern concerns the type of resources on which the plan consciously attempts to put the greatest emphasis. This pattern could be analysed, very roughly, into the human resources and the natural-resources approach to development.

It would, of course, be quite wrong to assume that emphasis on human resources implies lack of awareness of the importance of the natural resources or vice versa. Thus in Kenya's *Interim Report on Development of 1945*, in which insistence on the importance of natural resources has possibly been taken further than in any other development plan, Chapter III is entitled 'The People', and in it it is stated that 'the people cannot make a full contribution to output unless they are healthy and sufficiently well educated to understand the issues at stake. Health measures alone are insufficient. They must be preceded, accompanied and followed by education'.[1] In the same way a great deal of attention is paid to natural resources throughout every single development plan, however much the stated emphasis might have been on the human resources.

The difference between development plans from these points of view is, in fact, only one of emphasis; sometimes it seems almost to be one of drafting. Though it would be idle to try and compare provisions made for the various sectors in different development plans, with their greatly varying circumstances, it is not easy to dismiss the thought that their ultimate details may not have been greatly different whether their explicit emphasis had been on natural or on human resources. It is, in other words, quite possible that whatever the angle of approach to planning at a certain moment in a certain territory, the facts of the case, in which must be included both

[1] Cf. para. 18.

the general needs and resources of the community and the composition and past experience of the planning and executive administration, may well have led to closely similar results.

Nevertheless, the classification of the plans according to whether their emphasis is on natural or on human resources is not only formally valid, it can also be enlightening if account is taken of the background data. Especially interesting is the case in which the attitude within a territory changes because of fairly radical economic, administrative or political changes, but comparisons between different territories can also be useful especially when such territories are rather dissimilar.

In the matter of human resources Central Africa seems to stand out as especially conscious of the problems of labour inefficiency. Already in 1937 there had been an exhaustive enquiry into the supply and welfare of native labour in Tanganyika. The main conclusions of that enquiry had been that there was ample manpower for the needs of the territory but that from one cause and another there was a serious wastage of labour.

Major G. St J. Orde-Browne, the Labour Adviser to the Secretary of State, agreed in 1945 with the 1937 conclusions and gave as the main reasons for the wastage the 'deplorably low standard of efficiency of the worker' which he thought had been only accentuated by war conditions.[1] The Tanganyika Planning Commission went further and concluded that that low standard of efficiency was due to the lack of a 'spark of incentive' on the part of the average African, and that 'unless a way can be found to strike that spark the further development of the Territory is likely to be seriously impeded'.[2]

The Northern Rhodesian emphasis in its discussion of human resources was both on the importance of the social services and on the need for co-operation between the population and the administration:

'The development of the so-called social services that give better health or better skills, that will enable the manpower of the Territory to be used to the best advantage, is inevitable and entirely complementary to economic development; and no excuse is offered, therefore, for the inclusion in this review, which was originally ordained to be strictly "economic", of the modified

[1] Cf. *Report on Labour Conditions in East Africa*, November 22, 1945, para. 34.
[2] Cf. *A Ten Year Development and Welfare Plan for Tanganyika Territory*, 1946, para. 47.

development programmes of the Health Department and the two Education Departments.[1]

'Balanced development consists of an upward flow of ideas from the rural areas through the Native Authorities to Government and a complementary flow of services from Government to village Africans to assist them in their advancement. The critical point at which success or failure is likely to be determined is the point of contact between the European Government and the developing African.'[2]

In Uganda Mr Worthington put the problem much more tersely in his development plan: '... the vicious circle which depends upon lack of education-malnutrition-disease-inefficient work-low production must be broken at some point.'[3] Mr Worthington's analysis was enlarged upon by the Agricultural Productivity Committee, in 1954, in ways reminiscent of the Northern Rhodesian approach of 1948:

'We consider that investment in people through education and technical training in their various forms should in general have priority over investment in material resources; capital equipment and fertile land are wasted if they are not used with skill and efficiency. The growth of new skills and aptitudes is inevitably slow; it does not depend merely on the acquisition of new knowledge but on new standards of work and efficiency which must be grafted on to the existing social and economic heritage. Although the importation of "know-how" from abroad and programmes of research in Uganda will lay the foundation for the diffusion of new knowledge and techniques, they are no substitute for the laborious process of enlarging the peoples' intellectual horizon, raising their general standards of skills and, most important, increasing the range and the intensity of their wants.'[4]

Though the importance of human resources for economic development has thus been acknowledged in quite a few instances no attempt seems to have been made even at a guess at their relative contribution to such development as compared to a planned investment in material resources. Such acknowledgement has therefore been little more than a graceful bowing to strong feelings or beliefs or, in

[1] Cf. *Review of the Ten Year Development Plan*, 1948, para. 5.
[2] Cf. *Ten Year Development Plan for Northern Rhodesia*, 1948, para. 162.
[3] Cf. *A Development Plan for Uganda*, 1946, para. 143.
[4] Cf. *Report of the Agricultural Productivity Committee*, 1954, para. 15.

certain cases, an added argument for the use of funds for welfare purposes for which the main justification has been of a more directly humanitarian kind.

After the polite acknowledgment of the contributions to economic development an investment in human resources could make, the development plans have always settled down to the real business in hand, which has been investment for the purpose of the development of natural resources.

In the British and Belgian territories the emphasis has been mainly on the known natural resources, mineral prospecting (as well as exploitation) being often tacitly considered, though nowhere explicitly stated, to be largely the business of private investors. In the French territories the importance attached to geological investigations under development plans has on the whole loomed larger. But all plans have in fact concentrated most of their efforts on the provision of what was considered to be the necessary framework for the development of their natural resources, especially in connection with the establishment of communications and of other public works, such as water or power supplies, considered essential for agricultural and industrial development. When a more direct participation in the solution of the problems of production has been envisaged this has usually been connected with what might be called defensive measures, such as campaigns against soil erosion, cattle epidemics and the tsetse fly in the case of agriculture, and such as protective, or 'pioneer industries', measures in the case of industrial development. This prevalent defensive attitude in the sphere of production could not, on the whole,[1] be criticized for what it has been attempting to do, which has generally been necessary and useful; when criticisms have been put forward they have usually been in connection with what it has not attempted to tackle.

Priority Patterns in the Social Services: Extension versus Quality. The planning pattern which seems to emerge most clearly in the case of

[1] In the case of Kenya the preoccupation with the defence of the land had at a certain stage of planning, and having in view Kenya's particular conditions, gone possibly too far: 'We consider that it is of fundamental importance that the land should not be regarded as owned by several million individuals, each with his patch, large or small, which he is at liberty to destroy or develop as he thinks fit, but as something which is in a very real sense the property of the community as a whole and which the individual landholder, black, white or brown, holds in trust for his community. It is at once a heritage and a legacy—a heritage from the past and a legacy to the future—and the principle should be accepted that individual *ownership* rights should extend only as long as the owners are in beneficial occupation of their holding' (*The Interim Report on Development*, Kenya, 1945, chap. 2, 'Natural Resources', para. 14). (Author's italics.)

the social services concerns the possibility of an emphasis either on quality or an extension, and though this antithesis is not necessarily always correct, it may be taken as a working first approximation. This emphasis is, of course, doubly relative: the expansion to be undertaken, whether to a higher standard or to a wider diffusion, has to be compared both to the state of the services in the territory at the beginning of the plan and to their state in other, similar or model, communities.

A case for widely spread services at low cost per head argued in terms of the needs of a programme of economic development was made in Kenya. The proper utilization of manpower was taken to imply the development of 'adequate but not luxurious' health services and education, in particular the education of African children of both sexes and the mass education of African adults to the stage at which they could understand, at least in part, the problems which modern conditions create. The Development Committee stressed the point that 'unless the African mind could be brought to the pitch of being able to comprehend the broad requirements of a rehabilitation and development programme' and, more particularly, unless the principle that 'all must work' could be brought before the African in a convincing and effective way, there was no alternative to economic disaster. The committee felt that one of the most rapid ways of furthering economic development was therefore to give a measure of education to the illiterate and to provide technical and vocational training for a suitable minority of all races.[1]

A little later Northern Rhodesia put forward a plan which was couched in less utilitarian terms, proposing to 'give on a modest scale the bare essentials of social and economic services which all sections of the community require'.[2]

In contrast to this low standard, wide extension, approach in East and Central Africa could be quoted that of British West Africa, where there has been a tendency towards the spending of a fairly high proportion of the development funds on a comparatively small number of high-quality services (such as well-equipped hospitals and higher educational institutions) whose contribution to economic development is sometimes less easy to see. This approach is well summarized by the statement sometimes attributed to Dr Aggrey of the Gold Coast and which public figures, both in politics and outside,

---

[1] Cf. *Report of the Development Committee*, vol. i, 1946, para. 30. Nevertheless, this did not really change Kenya's insistence on the greater importance of natural resources for economic development.
[2] Cf. *Ten Year Development Plan for Northern Rhodesia*, 1948, para. 25.

often like to quote, that 'only the best is good enough for West Africa'. The balancing of quality and extension is, in fact, difficult both to define and to achieve.

The alternatives of widespread services at low cost per unit and of restricted and high-cost services have an additional, though not strictly derivative, implication concerning their location: expensive services tend to gravitate to the towns. The tendency of priority for urban development exists whatever the circumstances, but a concentration on costly services greatly strengthens this tendency, with obvious economic implications, as the pattern thus often becomes one of urban versus rural development.

CHAPTER 15

Some Individual Priorities

THE individual priority decisions range themselves within these patterns, often cutting across them. Of the 'purely' economic priorities, communications tend to have the greatest share in the development plans, with agriculture normally second, though their relative importance varies greatly from territory to territory and sometimes even from plan to plan within the same territory. On the social-services side education has almost always first place, with health normally following at some distance. In many territories the plan could almost be summarized as communications and education without missing out more than a small percentage of the total expenditure foreseen under it.

The problems raised by communications, having been repeatedly discussed and dealt with in the past, tend to appear fairly simple and to a large extent technical. The problems raised within the educational field tend to be seen chiefly in the semi-technical light of the possibilities for expansion in view of the available personnel and funds. Though education can provide subject for debates among the population concerned, such debates tend to restrict themselves to a fairly emotional discussion of the allocation of funds, especially as between education and other sectors, discussion which does not take much space in a development plan in its published form. In other words, though communications and education tend to be the main items of expenditure under development plans, they are sometimes discussed and analysed within the plans less than the remaining minor, but more controversial or doubtful, items. This tends to give development plans a much more 'balanced', in the sense of more widely spread, appearance than is warranted by their financial provisions.

The discussion below will be restricted to the two main economic items of development expenditure under the plans, communications and agriculture.

COMMUNICATIONS

Good communications are the absolutely essential foundation for a centralized administration, especially when such administration has only a small number of personnel at its disposal and must control very wide geographical areas. In all colonial expansions the first effective measures for taking over control, for 'pacification', have been the building of roads or railways. Though this aspect of road building still exists today,[1] it has lost much of its former importance, especially in the colonial territories with which this work deals, mainly because there are already sufficient roads, railways and airfields to meet most of the merely strategic or administrative needs of such territories.

The most important arguments advanced today in favour of the further development of communications are therefore economic arguments. Such arguments may be stated in a vague, general form, simply affirming that communications are good for the economy or the development of the country. 'We are firmly of the opinion that a better road system is vital to pave the way for more rapid development' and 'We have referred to the fact that in many fields of development we can do no more than attempt to keep pace with developments already taking place. By improving communications, on the other hand, we believe that a real impetus can be given to further development which should result in the strengthening of the colony's economy'.[2] '. . . the main roads of the Territory are in most cases incapable of carrying efficiently and through all weather the present traffic, let alone the increase expected from development. In any event, as regards roads it seemed that they were one of the much-needed improvements that could be got on with immediately, thanks to the increasing availability in the Territory of civil engineering contractors equipped with modern mechanical road plant, and that roads represented a lasting and visible physical asset which at the same time was essential to development.'[3] '. . . no less than 56 per cent of the total capital programme is devoted to communications of all kinds, in the belief that this aspect of its [the Federal Govern-

---

[1] Cf. 'For reasons of security and good administration high priority is recommended for the completion of the Elgon high-level road Kyesoweri-Bukwa, and the initiation of the roads Nabiswa-Namalu and Namalu-Karita. The former would provide also a cheap eastern outlet for economic crops via Kitale. The latter would relate closer administration and prevention of tribal affrays to the Governor's plans for the rehabilitation of Karammoja' (Uganda: *Five Year Capital Development Plan, 1955–60*, para. 57).
[2] Kenya: *Report of the Planning Committee, 1951*, paras. 104, 117.
[3] *Review of the Ten Year Development Plan of Northern Rhodesia*, 1948, para. 4.

SOME INDIVIDUAL PRIORITIES

ment's] constitutional responsibilities provides the greatest opportunity for a decisive advance in economic development.'[1]

When the arguments in favour of better communications are put forward in a more detailed form they can usually be classified into one or the other of two types. The first is that the new communications are necessary to meet existing needs. The second is that they are necessary to further the development of a stagnant economy. The usual implication of the second point is that such development will foster the creation of sufficient future transport needs to lead ultimately to the full utilization of the new communications. Both points are very succinctly made by Sir Alexander Gibb:[2] 'In mineral and industrial development involving heavy capital investments the provision of adequate transport facilities is regarded as an essential part of the project. The gold of the Transvaal, the chrome, asbestos and coal of Southern Rhodesia, the zinc and lead of Northern Rhodesia, and the copper of the Katanga called for and secured the necessary railway construction' (Point 1). 'In areas, however, where development must essentially be based on a gradually improving or expanding agriculture, the demand for transport facilities is different. Here the provision of transport must usually precede development and an initial idle period be allowed for as part of the price of opening the gate to agricultural progress' (Point 2).

The first type of argument may be analysed into three main cases. The first, most widespread and most straightforward of the three cases, involves the need for an improvement in the standards of existing communications—roads, railways, harbours, etc.—to cope with an increase in traffic which has already taken place. This was especially important in the first development plans in view of wartime neglect and deteriorations, and it continued to have pride of place following the rapid expansion of the movement of goods and passengers along existing axes of communications which followed on the rapid economic expansion of the post-war days. It has involved widening and straightening of roads, widening and strengthening of bridges and culverts, improvements in surfacing and sometimes, especially in the case of the Belgian Congo and, more rarely, in that of the British territories, in the road foundations. It has also involved improvements in river crossings, either by better ferry arrangements including night-workings or by the replacement of ferries by

[1] *The Economic Programme of the Government of the Federation of Nigeria, 1955–60*, 1956, para. 203.
[2] Cf. *Report on Central African Rail Link Development Survey*, 1952, vol. i, p. 27, para. 3, chapter headed 'Available and Potential Traffic'.

bridges. In the case of railways it has involved a strengthening of foundations, replacement of existing rails with heavier types, improvement in rolling-stock including a gradual introduction of diesel engines, especially important over the long distances in the French African territories and, in certain cases, the doubling of railway tracks. Much work has also been done on the extension and re-equipment of harbours. Though the introduction of new railway transport for the solution of the problems of a traffic which had become too heavy for the road system has also often been suggested it has usually been due, when actually implemented, to more complex causes.

The second case, closely connected with the first, has been the construction of short-cuts connecting two regions whose direct trading relations have increased sufficiently to make their existing communications via a third region, which in the past may have acted as their common market and source of supplies, economically unsatisfactory. This second case may vary in importance and significance from the construction of links of a few miles, at low standards and costs, to first-class roads or rail links involving major works of art and costing millions of pounds. Unfortunately, such short-cuts tend to be administratively and aesthetically very satisfying and their economic justification may sometimes be much smaller than that advanced.

The third case, which may be loosely identified with that of the feeder roads, involves the connection with the main network of communications of areas which have developed rapidly. It usually involves short links, at fairly low standards, to connect small populations to their markets, but, as the number of such units tends to be very large, the feeder roads constitute a very important aspect of transport development.

Theoretically it is possible to envisage, as a fourth case, the need for a major link connecting two large and economically active regions which had so far been isolated and where there is an obvious pent-up demand for transport facilities sufficient to justify such a link. In practice, with the exception of major mining discoveries such that they can be economically exploited even if the costs of establishing new transport links with the world markets are included, such cases are difficult to discover.

In connection with the second type of economic argument, which concerns the development of economically stagnant areas, railways seem to have been especially popular in administrative circles[1] but

---

[1] e.g. The projected East Africa Rail Link, Gold Coast Northern Territories Railway, Nigerian North-Eastern (Bornu-Chad) extension, the French Niger links, for most of which more sober views have ultimately prevailed.

roads, if of a sufficiently high standard, have also been acceptable. The results of such projects when actually carried out seem so far to have been almost uniformly disappointing, from the pre-war trans-Zambesi railway and the French Sudan ventures to the more recent attempts, as in French Equatorial Africa or in the Upper Volta. The importance of establishing new means of communications to connect isolated areas with wider markets must not be underrated as an incentive to development, but there are indications that the problem has tended to be bedevilled by the utterly uneconomic insistence on entertaining only high-cost type of investments for long-distance axes of communications, probably along the line of argument that standards of construction must vary with the length of the link, density of traffic being of secondary importance in such decisions.

Sometimes the two types of economic arguments in favour of improved or of new axes of communications are used together, especially where the existing quantitative information on transport needs is not considered to have given a full picture of the problem. Such a mixed economic argument, interesting because it deals with two adjoining stretches of road, was included in the Uganda Plan:

> 'Road traffic surveys carried out early in 1954 show that the *volume of traffic is heavier* on the Kampala–Gayaza–Burgere road than on any other stretches of main road in the kingdom. It is accordingly recommended that the first part of this road—that is to say Kampala to Gayaza—should have the highest priority in Buganda for survey and reconstruction, and that in due course consideration should be given to further works carrying the road onwards from Gayaza across the Sezibwa River to Kayunga in Bugere, an area of *rapidly increasing agricultural importance*. The Council, moreover, does not exclude the future possibility of the construction of a road bridge or a mechanized ferry service over the Nile from somewhere opposite Mbulamuti or Luzinga, which would provide this important area with an easily accessible railhead.'[1]

Administrative and other arguments, such as of a prestige or political character, can also be adduced, transforming the communication axis under discussion literally into a multi-purpose project.[2]

[1] Uganda: *Five Year Capital Development Plan, 1955–60*, para. 56. Author's italics.
[2] A good example of such a mixed project is to be found in the already quoted extract from the Uganda Plan—see p. 164, fn.

The tendency of colonial populations to form into discrete groups spatially separated from each other as well as from the world markets may be taken as another starting-point for an analysis of communication problems and policies. This approach leads to results similar to those already indicated and in certain instances even to a repetition of the previous arguments. It can, nevertheless, throw a certain amount of additional light on the problem of communications as a whole. A number of cases may be distinguished.

The first case, historically and in order of importance, is the linking of a local group with the world market. This applies especially to communities near the sea.

The almost unanimous experience since the last world war in matters of communications has been that, however bold or even rash projects of new harbours or of harbour extensions have seemed to be, events have tended not only to justify them but even to leave them behind. Even in the French Union, where planned expenditure on transport has been extremely high and has as a whole proved disappointingly uneconomic,[1] ports have proved a notable exception. This is, of course, connected with the whole tendency towards rapid post-war development of the colonies due to increased world demand and increased prices for raw-materials. Though it does, therefore, not mean that an 'artificial' harbour development before the war, or a 'forced' harbour development in the future, would have coincided or will necessarily coincide with increased needs for such harbours, this recent experience does emphasize the prior importance in the development of such territories of their links with the world markets.

The second case is that of a population group which is not only isolated from other groups within the colonial territory but is also at a great distance, economically speaking, from the outside world. The three million strong population in the neighbourhood of the Niger bend is one example, the populations in the highlands of East and Central Africa are other examples.

When such a population group is within an administrative territory more or less geographically limited to the extension of the main homogeneous group, its trade with the outside world and thus its possibilities of a specialization in cash products depends strictly on the profitability of these products, which must be able to bear the cost of their transport across the territories of other groups to the world markets. Such is the case with the coffee and cotton of Uganda or with the minerals and the tobacco of the Rhodesias.

---

[1] Cf. unanimous criticisms of the first plan of development by both the majority and the minority reports and proposals on the second plan.

In other cases, such as those already quoted of the French Union, those now being discussed of the Bornu-Chad region in Nigeria, or those for whose sake have been put forward the proposals for a central African link, there can be a strong clash between the economic and the political aspects of the problem. The tendency to sweep away economic considerations in favour of the administrative-political fetish (applied out of its context) of equality of opportunity to all groups within a territory can lead to undertakings which may impose a heavy financial or economic burden on the geographical population groups whose activities are more profitable without an equivalent increase in overall returns to the benefiting, subsidized, populations, let alone to the area under unitary administrative control as a whole.

The third case is that of the attraction towards one of the specializing population groups which has entered international trade of the surrounding groups for whose surplus products, usually food, the specializing, cash product, central group is now becoming a customer. This normally involves a movement of foodstuffs towards the centre and of imported goods outwards, and very often leads also to a movement of population, both for farming purposes and as labourers, from the satellite groupings towards the centre.

The fourth case is that of a number of communities in fairly close geographical proximity to each other but which economically are connected neither with each other nor with the world at large. Their problem is more complicated because there are two measures to be taken which are both necessary but whose precedence in time is difficult to decide upon: to enable the creation of a local market wide enough to facilitate local specialization the individual communities must be connected with each other; and the larger community thus being created must be connected with the outside world. This case seems to be of special importance in Tanganyika and in parts of Kenya, but it exists in various degrees and for various-sized communities throughout the larger of the colonial territories.

The fifth and the sixth cases are complementary. The fifth case, which is in many ways an extension of the third, concerns a population group whose conditions of distance from potential markets are such that the sale of its products would be uneconomic, but which can move *en bloc* towards economically better surroundings. In other words, it involves the possibility of the transportation of the population towards the existing centres of activity as an alternative to the creation of an uneconomic permanent communication link.

Such movements take place continuously over short distances, in which case the economic and social surrounds into which the populations move are not very dissimilar to those they left behind. They also take place in the heavy movements from rural to urban areas which involve a radical change in social habits and in systems of production. And they also take place over much longer distances, often in search of better natural resources for the carrying out of traditional activities, as in the case of the permanently migrant fishermen of West Africa, or of the cocoa farmers planting new farms in fairly distant and as yet unopened regions. The squatters in East and Central Africa are a similar phenomenon.

The sixth, and complementary, case is the setting up of productive activities with heavy capital investments in uninhabited territories, usually in connection with mineral exploitation, and the introduction of populations from outside to provide labour and later on supplies of foodstuffs and of other necessaries for the labour force.

The past tendency throughout the South and Central African mining areas as well as in West Africa of relying on migrant labour for such purposes and not on stable populations is beginning to be thought an expensive way of dealing with this problem. The Belgian experiments undertaken over the last few years of bringing in families to the Upper Katanga mines from the fairly distant Ruanda-Urundi, instead of bringing in migrant workers, have led to a drastic fall in labour turnover, to a high increase in labour efficiency and to the solution of additional problems through the better local food production, as a result of the activities of the miners' families, and through some diversification of the economy. It has also, obviously, led to an increasing need for schools and housing, but the rapidly increasing reliance of the Belgian mining companies on this type of recruitment indicates that they find the overall balance of profit definitely in its favour.

AGRICULTURE

There is general agreement that agriculture must be developed, but there has been a fair amount of variation in the views expressed both on the possibilities of such development and on the best methods to be used. Specific development schemes have depended largely upon local conditions, involving climate, soils, populations and markets. Certain general approaches may nevertheless be traced.

One is the large-scale mechanized project approach. The consistent failures of large-scale mechanized projects have continued over a number of years but some are still being run both in the French and

British, West and East African, territories as well as in Surinam. They have been appreciably whittled down and have become chiefly experimental projects, but they indicate that there is at least still some faith in the possibilities of the mechanization idea for tropical regions.

Even in Tanganyika, where the blow of the failure of the Kongwa scheme has been especially violent, experiments are still being continued in the hope and belief that the production of African food crops should be capable of increase by the application of mechanized aids. Large-scale pilot schemes have been undertaken in the Rufiji Valley for rice production and in the Lake Province for sorghum, millet and cotton production. The 'economic balance between hire charges, costs and tractor usage' has still not been found, but it is felt that experience is at least showing certain basic requirements for the success of such schemes. A parallel development has been in the provision of mechanized aids to tenant farmers on Overseas Food Corporation farms at Nachingwea.[1]

The possible exception to these series of failures may be the schemes combining irrigation with large-scale mechanization, and recalling, though not necessarily imitating, the Sudan Gezira scheme. The French Sudan Niger bend (or inner delta) project may prove ultimately to be such an exception.

Partly as a reaction to such failures, partly from more direct considerations, increasing emphasis is being put today on the opposite approach, that of cautious and gradual improvements to the existing types of peasant agriculture. This changed approach has been spreading slowly but fairly steadily and has already become generally accepted in Surinam, in British East Africa, in the West Indies as well as in the French, and to a fair extent the Belgian, territories.

In Uganda, which had never been very happy about large-scale projects, the Agricultural Productivity Committee has put forward plans which do not involve heavy capital expenditure, explaining that it did not believe that that was the best way by which the 'vital enhancement' of agricultural activity could be obtained. It proposed instead a steady increase in scope and extent of existing activities, which are essentially and necessarily recurrent activities, and which both the Development Council and the Productivity Committee believed to be the decisive factor.[2] The committee included among such activities 'investment in people' through education and technical

[1] Cf. *Tanganyika Annual Report for 1953*, 1954, para. 17.
[2] Cf. Uganda: *Five Year Capital Development Plan, 1955–60*, para. 113(a).

training, which they felt ought in general to have priority over investment in material resources.[1]

Similar views to those in Uganda were put forward, in more detail, in the Swynnerton Report in Kenya.[2] This report pointed out that the agricultural and land development schemes fostered under the previous ten-year development plan which had made the biggest contribution to development were not the more spectacular projects in which large sums of money had been invested but which had only touched the fringe of the agricultural problem, but those which had augmented and intensified the 'old established and experienced services' of the Government, e.g. the Soil Conservation (African Areas) Scheme, the Agricultural Research and Investigation Scheme, the Livestock Improvement Scheme, and Tsetse Survey and Control.[3] Swynnerton's recommendations may in fact be roughly summarized as the development of cash crops based on improved peasant cultivation.

Of course, there has always been awareness of the need for improving peasant agriculture, though probably more emphatically so in the West Indies, where the high ratio of people to land has presented less of a temptation for extensive mechanization than in the vaster and more sparsely inhabited African territories. In Jamaica, where economic, social and population problems are probably as difficult as anywhere in the colonies, the 1945 Development Plan emphasized the paramount importance of improvements of agricultural methods, of an intensified use of the land (including measures to prevent soil erosion), of the extension of land settlement and of the encouragement of mixed farming.[4] But the tendency in matters of the encouragement of peasant farming seems to have been for a long time to follow a shoe-string policy.

The significant part about the more recent developments has been an increase in the scope of the administrations' efforts, including even large-scale experiments in new types of smallholdings.

In Northern Rhodesia, for example, to attain the stated main aim and long-term objective of the Rural Development Plan for African areas of bringing about an improvement in the African system of agriculture, peasant-farming schemes have been tried out in several districts. The results in Fort Jameson having been considered to have proved that, in suitable areas, African smallholders could make a

---

[1] Cf. *Report of the Agricultural Productivity Committee*, para. 15.
[2] Cf. *A Plan to Intensify the Development of African Agriculture in Kenya*, 1954.
[3] Cf. *op. cit.*, para. 89.
[4] *A Ten Year Plan of Development for Jamaica*, 1945, para. 111.

good living from the soil using methods designed to preserve its fertility, a scheme has been drawn up, covering a period of ten years, for the expansion of peasant farming with the intention of establishing some four thousand new peasant farms during that period.[1]

Improvements in agricultural output based on the development of peasant agriculture tend to concentrate on better methods of cultivation and on a better choice of crops, both of which depend on improved knowledge and, especially, on methods of passing on this knowledge successfully to the farmers. It is especially in this last aspect that agricultural development plans based on peasant cultivation seem to have most often tended to get bogged down. The main problems seem to have been the lack of the right kind of personnel in sufficient numbers, and the difficulty of finding the most suitable crop, the last problem being often bedevilled by attempts at self-sufficiency.

Compromises between large-scale schemes and individual peasant schemes have also been attempted, either in the form of plantations, which have often proved successful, as in the Cameroons and in the Ivory Coast, or on the lines of the introduction over large areas of peasant cash crops with extensive advisory and marketing facilities, as in Northern Rhodesia for tobacco and more recently in Kenya for pyrethrum, coffee and pineapples. Such a combined system of widespread individual cash-crop growing plus large-scale services has had the added advantage that it has tended to facilitate the introduction of some measure of local processing, leading towards a more intensive use of local labour resources.

[1] Cf. *Revision of the Northern Rhodesia Ten Year Development Plan*, 1953, para. 37.

PART VI

CONCLUSIONS

CHAPTER 16

Conclusions

THE analysis attempted in the course of this book cannot be said to have revealed any striking new facts or interpretations in connection with development planning in the colonial territories surveyed. What it seems to have succeeded in emphasising are the obvious truths that planning is mainly an administrative exercise; that administrations, even when reluctant at first to look ahead for more than the budgetary year, have grown (though sometimes slowly) to appreciate the advantages of exercises in longer-term budgeting; and that the success of planning depends on the quality and status of the planners.

It was stated in Chapter 1 that the differences between individual development plans in the colonial territories are too great to allow of quantitative comparisons or of aggregation. The analysis attempted in the subsequent chapters should have made it apparent that, in addition, each individual plan has undergone appreciable changes in course of execution, so that there may be little resemblance even between one and the same plan as originally conceived, and published, and as finally implemented.

This need not imply a criticism of colonial planning as opposed to planning elsewhere. In the Soviet Union, where conditions for planning are as near ideal as possible, the whole economic, political and social life having been shaped to facilitate planning; where non-planned home activities have been reduced to a minimum and their unforeseeable impacts on the planned sphere practically eliminated; where the home economy is almost completely insulated from demand and supply changes in the outside world; the plans *ex post* tend to differ appreciably from *ex ante*.

The persistent under-estimation by the Soviet planners of development under their five-year plans is not, of course, taken here to imply an inability to make accurate forecasts. After thirty years of planning experience the Soviet planners should be able, if they so wanted, to make fairly close overall estimates of results under their plans. They should even be able to make allowances by now for such non-quantitative elements as "mass enthusiasm for the plan". The "five-year plan in four years" is not inaccurate planning. The plans in U.S.S.R. having been transformed into national campaigns, a battle psychosis is essential, and there is nothing more depressing in a war than to see your target receding out of grasp, and nothing more exhilarating than to be ahead of schedule. A break-through can push an army—and a nation—to a fever pitch of activity. An underestimation of future results is thus good psychology.

But if the official overall underestimation must be regarded as a matter of policy and should not be attributed to any deficiency in the planning machinery, the distortions within the plan obviously must. A twenty per cent increase in every sector (plus or minus the allowable small variations for a balanced plan at the higher level) is one thing, an average twenty per cent increase which hides hundred per cent increases in some sectors and nil increases in others, as has been the case in all Soviet plans, is a different matter. Results in the second case have obviously escaped the control of the planners.

Colonial planning has been nowhere near that complete control of all aspects of economic life available to the Soviet planners. The variables outside its control have been many and their effect often decisive. With a restricted field of action, colonial planning could not emulate the Soviets in a planning of production. It could only tackle some of the tools of production. It could provide some of the means, but could seldom make any attempt to estimate, let alone control or ensure the results, in terms of national output, from such means.

Keeping in mind the obvious impossibility, under such conditions, of planning with any degree of accuracy, it is still important, in a discussion of the scope and effects of the plans, to distinguish between some of the flights of fancy in which certain plans— especially some of the earlier ones—have indulged, and the proposals contained in plans which it has actually proved possible to implement. The realistic plans have all been based on well-established administrative experience, and have dealt with recognized administrative functions.

The relationship between the planning machinery and the plan is reciprocal: a plan will only be able to cover efficiently those items which an existing planning machinery is fitted to cope with; in the same way, a planning machinery, to be effective, must be adjusted in every instance to the scope of the plan. A development of the planning machinery as the result of increased experience can thus enlarge the sphere of effective planning and, on the other hand, an increasing desire by the community or by its effective mouthpieces, either political or administrative, for planned development will lead to a strengthening of the machinery. The process can be one of give-and-take and possibly, though not necessarily, a cumulative one. It certainly seems to have been in the instances of recent colonial experience a gradual one, including a fair amount of back-slipping, if not actually of back-pedalling.

Plans, their contents, and their effects have varied from colony to colony. General appreciations have therefore of necessity to deal with rather vague overall concepts. Nevertheless it should be possible to discern some kind of an outline, however blurred or shifting, of what plans may have succeeded in achieving, of what they have done but may have done wrongly, and of what they have omitted to do.

THE NON-CONTROVERSIAL ACHIEVEMENTS OF THE PLANS

Within a highly unstable colonial administrative framework and with frequent changes within an insufficient personnel, plans have often succeeded in providing some kind of fixed schema of activities to which successive intakes into each territory's administration could refer. Though plans cannot provide a complete solution to the problems raised by the rapid transfers of personnel, they have been able in certain cases to provide at least a partial remedy. In other cases the plans have unfortunately not proved a sufficiently powerful means of providing continuity, and with the addition of rapidly changing general economic conditions the plans have been relegated to polite but effective pigeon-holing. This pigeon-holing has nevertheless become increasingly difficult as the habit of having a plan around the place has begun to take root, and appreciation of the continuity-providing function of a plan has been steadily increasing.

The plans have also enabled—or forced—the administrations to take a wider view of their own tasks, and this in two ways: by making them look ahead not only for one year, as is the normal custom under an annual budgetary system, but for a period of years; and by making it necessary for them to give at least the impression of some co-ordination of the various individual tasks so far undertaken by isolated departments. The habit of planning has thus brought about a more integrated approach by each administration to its normal problems, and has enabled it to put them in better perspective.

The plans have finally succeeded in making administrations 'development conscious' in a much more radical manner than they had ever been before. Administrations were still haunted immediately after the war by the stringency of the war and pre-war periods, and there is little doubt that it might have taken them much longer to gather enough courage to embark upon development projects if there had not been in existence the continuous reminder of the plans.

More recently, as development plans have begun to be more widely known throughout the respective populations, and as some of the results which could be ascribed to them have begun to be seen and felt, there has also arisen an increasing interest among members of the population in the possibilities of planned co-operation for purposes of development.

THE CONTROVERSIAL ASPECTS OF THE PLANS

There are few items in colonial plans which have not been vigorously criticized at some time or other as sins of commission or of omission. The criticisms of *content* have concerned either the scope of the plan, or the relative weights within the plan. The criticisms of *form* have concerned the methods of raising resources, the methods of disbursing them, and the efficiency of the planning and implementing machinery.

Criticisms of Content. Development plans are today a feature not only in most of the colonial territories but in an increasingly large number of self-governing countries as well. Criticisms of the *scope* of plans in the colonies tend therefore to be made on the basis of examples drawn from all over the world. In these examples the proportion of the total activities of the community which are covered by a plan varies greatly, from the totalitarian approach of communist countries, through the socializing tendencies of others, to a planning which involves little more than longer-period budgeting for the strictly administrative needs of central governments of a liberal-capitalist type.

Arguments in favour of an increase in the sphere of planning—making abstraction of purely doctrinaire arguments—are usually based on the twin views that private capital investment is low in poor countries, and that the possibilities of centrally guided development are much better than in the rich countries because the path of development up to that standard is already known. Arguments against a spread of planning deny that planned investment can in reality be more productive, because it tends to be undertaken in big gulps, whereas what is needed are small doses which are best given on an individual, non-planned, basis. They also deny that the paths already trodden by today's rich countries are necessarily either relevant, or possible, or the best for the colonies. It is not easy to adduce proofs for either type of contention. A combination of public investment and of individual employment of it—as for example in widely spread but small agricultural schemes based on gradual improvements through the use of new crops and of short-term investments like fertilizers or better tools—such as is now being increasingly put forward as an alternative solution, both by outside specialists and by some of the administrations, may well provide a fruitful compromise.

Criticisms of the *relative weights* within the plans will obviously always exist, and few of them could be discussed without a detailed knowledge of all the facts of each case, though even then it would be idle to expect much in the way of general agreement. Nevertheless, there is one classification common to most colonial plans which is at least debatable from the economic point of view and which is of a sufficiently general character to be discussed here. It is that into an economic and a social-services sector.

Lip service has indeed been paid in certain plans as well as in certain metropolitan pronouncements to the effect improvements in social services can have in the economic sphere. But, except in some of those cases in which attempts have been made to deal with the planning of economic development on a problem basis, there has been a fairly clear-cut division between the economic and the social-welfare sectors. The unstated argument in favour of such a division seems to be that, of all the factors of production involved, the human factor is the least likely to yield an economic return to investments of the type which can be undertaken or fostered by a centrally drafted development plan. Social services tend therefore to be regarded either as a political need or as a human right, but from the economic point of view they are normally considered as providing only consumption goods and services. There is much evidence today, provided by sociologists and anthropologists, by doctors and sanitation experts, as well as by industrial and agricultural enterprises working in the colonial territories and in similar territories elsewhere, that such may well not be the case and that comparatively small investments in human health, nutrition, education or community development, if properly conceived and carefully undertaken, may have an economic yield appreciably higher than investment in other spheres. Indeed, an economic argument based on generally accepted evidence could be put forward in favour of such views.

In the western high-income countries the basic conditions of health and education are comparatively good; and as the low-cost improvements in those spheres have already been carried out, any further improvements can only be undertaken at relatively high cost and low yield in economic terms. In the colonial territories, which are still far from this marginal position, it is possible, on the other hand, to use with great effect the cheapest of the methods and devices developed in the high-income communities, with a resultant high yield from the investments undertaken.

In fact the position is not quite so simple because of certain specific differences between the conditions in the two types of communities which have made some of the cheaper solutions devised in the western communities inapplicable in the tropics; but there is today at least a good approximation to it. There have, indeed, in recent times been rapid developments in that direction, some fostered by the health and nutritional needs of the troops fighting in the tropics and some by the need for rapid training in new skills arising out of war conditions, as well as out of rapid expansions in new types of production. In medicine, for example, it is possible today to do as much for endemic or epidemic human tropical diseases, such as malaria or yellow fever, as it has been possible to do for epizooties, such as rinderpest, or for plant diseases. It is rather ironical that while the latter are firmly accepted as of economic importance, medical measures, curative and preventive, which can appreciably increase the economic productivity of human beings are still consistently treated purely as social services. It is, therefore, difficult to accept the existing dichotomy into *economic* and *welfare* planning as economically valid in the present-day circumstances of the colonial territories.

This may have been the reason for the reclassification by the United Kingdom's Colonial Office of investments into those with an *immediate yield* and those with a *delayed or indefinite yield*. Unfortunately the tendency in the colonial territories has been to apply this reclassification only to the economic sphere. The result has been a further subdivision instead of a reconsideration and rearrangement of the whole field of planning.

Criticisms of Form. The methods of raising resources for the implementation of the plans are of importance because of the size of the plans' finances compared to the total investment funds within the territories. The danger is that, by an injudicious use of taxation in order to raise the largest possible amount of finance, the potentialities of small local investments are nullified. Measures are normally

CONCLUSIONS 183

taken to safeguard pioneer industries against such dangers, but these do not affect the small producer who cannot have recourse to any pioneer industry arrangements. The importance of pioneer industries for introducing new methods of manufacture and new products is great, but the rapid expansion of output which is the main desideratum will have to come about through the increased productivity of a very large number of well-established trades and industries, which would not qualify as pioneer. Especially undesirable is the ruthless taxation of the producers of cash crops —either direct taxation or through the device of marketing-board funds—which can prevent the healthy development of a middle class of small investors.

The methods of disbursing the resources are closely connected with the organization of the administrative machinery. The tendency, as already mentioned, has been to concentrate on few and large investments, which need little administrative staff, and which in addition are easy to see and to point out in the future as concrete examples of the benefits of planning. Programmes involving a multiplicity of small projects, cut down to the size of the possibilities of management and of recurrent-costs financing of the local population, have been less popular. Such programmes would need a large number of administrative staff to initiate them and to give the instructions and advice necessary during at least the first stages. With an increasing availability of local staff, which can be both more economical and more aware of local problems and possibilities, it should be possible to switch over more and more from the large-scale to the small but widely spread type of disbursements. This should also lessen the gap between taxation and the benefits from government activities now affecting cash-crop producers who in certain of the colonial territories are in fact financing the industrial projects. Under this new system such producers would themselves become more direct beneficiaries of planning and, in addition, part of the present regressive redistribution of income by taxation would become less necessary.

FUTURE POSSIBILITIES

The planning and implementing machineries have been creaking rather badly. Nobody could be said to be satisfied with them, least of all the respective administrations. There is, on the other hand, no clearcut solution under the existing systems to the problem of establishing efficient organizations. Planning depends too much on a changing personnel within a changing system of administration and of responsibilities. As a result the needs of a plan may often take second place to the needs of administrative reorganization, especially in connection with an increasing political participation by the local population in the affairs of the territory. Personal idiosyncrasies can also play an important role in small administrations where powerful personalities have a forceful impact on policy. Though the problems of planning and implementation which an administration has had to face and their administrative solutions can be discussed and classified, it is not possible for an outsider to do more than guess at the clash of personalities which may often have been the real reason for changes and variations which sometimes might appear logical and sometimes not.

Though there is still little agreement within the tropical dependencies on the best way of carrying out long-term planning of government expenditure, such planning seems nevertheless to have become a generally accepted method for speeding up their economic and social development. From the analysis so far undertaken here there seem to emerge a number of facts which ought to be taken into account if planning is to become an administratively convenient device, a materially effective exercise, and a psychologically useful method of promoting the necessary feeling of participation within the populations concerned.

Planning must be done in terms of as complete an analysis as possible of each of the problems to be solved. This involves, firstly, consultation between experts drawn from different departments. It also involves, in the second place, the need to take into consideration different periods of time to suit the different problems. Twenty years may indeed be too short, as the Moyne Commission implied, to deal with the development of agriculture or of education. On the other hand, eighteen months might be quite sufficient to establish a network of VHF communications. The attempt to impose a rigid time limit for a plan must therefore be avoided. The original Colonial Office concept of a ten-year plan in general outline, split up into five-year periods to be planned in detail as and when feasible, was a first approximation to a solution of this problem. But experience seems to have shown, as we have seen, that it is not good enough. The system developed after the first few years of planning in the Belgian Congo, by which the originally fairly detailed ten-year plan has been combined with a system of more realistic moving short-term plans of three years' duration, comes much closer to a solution. The Surinam attempts at basing the plan on a projection of population size, needs and potentialities fifteen years hence, and the similar, more recent, projections made by the French planners for Algeria and which take into account possible alternative capital concentrations, add useful methods of outlining the shape of the plans.

On the other hand, more refined attempts at sector analysis are almost certainly premature, the quantitatively measurable exchanges and relations between industries within these territories being still of comparatively small importance. The main exceptions are the contributions to the rest of the economy made by food production, transport, and by the reservoir of unskilled labour which is normally available in the agricultural sector, all of which can be fairly simply dealt with.

A plan should, in short, be developed along lines likely to provide the necessary popular appeal, say by giving a definite even though fairly distant target of increased national output. It should enable the administrative machine as such, as well as the rapidly changing successive generations of administrators and (in the increasing number of cases where political groups are now the ultimately deciding factor) the even more rapidly changing generations of politicians, to proceed with their development measures within a generally agreed and fairly stable framework of reference. Finally, it should permit short-term, flexible and at the same time realistic estimates of the work to be undertaken, of the resources available for it and of the liabilities involved.

Such planning could only be undertaken with some difficulty by the rudimentary administrations of the smaller of the tropical dependencies. Indeed, from this point of view smallness might be said to extend fairly high up the scale. The specialist teams needed for such exercises could in fact only be afforded by a very few territories. But there is no reason why each territory should have its own private specialist team. A peripatetic team, or teams, comparable to some extent to the increasingly popular O & M teams, and sponsored either by the respective metropolitan power, or on some joint basis by all the powers and territories involved, or even on a wider international scale, is not beyond the realms of practicability. Indeed, this seems to be the direction in which the French system may be moving at the moment and this is the way in which International Bank Missions have already to some extent been used. The establishment of a number of other *ad hoc* organisations, such as the United Nations' Economic Regional Commissions, the Commission for Technical Co-operation in Africa South of the Sahara, the Anglo-American Caribbean Commission, the Colombo Plan, may also be regarded as steps in the right direction, even though the functions of such organisations have so far been more of centralising information and of providing a forum for the exchange of views than of building up loanable teams of experts.

The creation, and the readiness to make use, of such teams would depend on a number of factors. It would depend on the availability of the type of specialists needed. It would depend on attractive conditions of work and pay, and hence on the financial means at the disposal of the teams. It would finally depend on their acceptability by the territories and countries involved.

It is the last condition which is the most difficult to meet in the case of planning teams. Planning is to such an extent a mixture of technique and politics that any outside advice can easily become 'outside interference'. The field of action of outside teams will therefore tend to be limited to what can be shown to the complete satisfaction of local political leaders as well as of local administrators to be 'purely technical' matters. Among the most important contributions of international organisations in the field of planned development will be the sifting of the technical problems of development from the political and, in time, the de-politicizing of an increasing number of sectors. Primary teaching may, at a certain stage of development, be a matter for political debate, at another a purely technical issue. Medical services, agricultural extension services, road-building programmes, even administrative re-organisations of a departmental or territorial type can thus move from one field to the other. If a community run by a bureaucracy is in danger of death by suffocation, one in which every issue is political is in danger of allowing passions to over-rule knowledge and judgment based on knowledge. Outside teams of experts will only be acceptable and useful where there is a compromise between these two extremes.

But if such teams might succeed in solving the problem of effective planning now facing most of the colonial territories, they would not be able to overcome the obstacles to economic and social development which are due to the very smallness, economically speaking, of these territories. The gross national products of France, of Germany and of the United Kingdom are each some three to four times as large as the total estimated national product of all the tropical dependencies discussed here taken together. If the European Common Market and the Free Trade Area are to-day considered essential to avoid a stifling of the economic development of Western Europe, it is out of tune with the times to think of such economically insignificant units as the Gambia, or even of the 'large' territories of Tanganyika or of French Equatorial Africa, as sufficiently important economically to be able to lift themselves by their own bootstraps. In matters of economic development small-time nationalism or territorialism must be accepted as out of date.

It may be useful to remember, in this context, that nationalism is a fairly limited concept, both spatially and temporally. A product mainly of the French Revolution and of German romanticism, it ravaged Europe for a century but its success in the rest of the world has been much more circumscribed. Its force as an expansionist agent (*pace* the Arab League) is spent. It is still important as an agent in the fight for self-determination, but it has not seemed able in recent years to survive for long its own success. The social, political, economic and educational problems of newly emerging self-governing states are hard facts which do not allow Governments or populations to continue long in conditions of emotional nationalism (how 'nationalist' is the Indian Congress to-day?) even where such states could fairly be called 'national' states. And few of to-day's colonial territories, or even of the independent countries until recently of colonial status, would qualify as such. For a sovereign country in a state of peace, nationalism in its separatist, isolationist aspects has become an expensive and unproductive—possibly even dangerous—luxury.

Territorialism does not have the emotional content of nationalism and thus does not even provide the emotional release of fulfilment. It easily breaks up into tribalism or regionalism of various kinds. Its administrative origins are seldom a sufficiently valid reason for its indefinite continuation. Sooner or later in the process of economic development it has to be overcome. How soon depends on the stage reached. The poorer the community, the lower its needs and its means of satisfying them, the smaller the territory needed for its economic activities. Increases in wealth go hand in hand with increases in territory, in the 'market'. If the growth of the market is prevented, the economy will stagnate. Within limits there can, of course, be growth within a circumscribed territory, both by drawing into the territorial market groups so far on the fringe, and by improving local techniques and capital equipment. Such growth can be quite vigorous at times, depending on a number of factors, such as the size of previously untapped local resources or the rapidity of acquisition and spread of new methods and techniques. But such spurts will seldom last long. Sooner or later, the need for wider markets than can be provided territorially will make itself felt.

The only real answer to this problem under present conditions is a close relationship with existing large and vigorous economies.

Existing geographical and economic factors seem to indicate some obvious connections. For the West Indies, the United States–Canada complex, with additional ties with Europe. For the African territories, the European Common Market and the Free Trade Area, with additional ties with the United States and Canada. For the South-East Asian and Pacific territories, the industrialised or industrialising countries of Australasia and the Asiatic mainland, with additional ties with Europe and America. The political problem of combining such economic co-operation, maybe even integration, with jealously guarded territorial independence is outside the scope of this work, but to-day it is less difficult to accept its feasibility than it was even ten years ago. Meanwhile co-operation, mostly of a technical but possibly also of an administrative character, between neighbouring colonial or former colonial territories could make future economic co-operation with more distant but economically more useful partners easier to accept both psychologically and politically.

Within the framework of such wider partnerships planning, if still felt to be useful, could be undertaken with a much more economical and efficient use of planning teams. On the greatly enlarged canvas which would thus be made available, it should be possible not only to combine the varied experience of officials and experts already in the field of colonial planning, but to draw upon the additional experience of the many other countries where 'planning' of administrative activities has now become an accepted feature. The relevance to colonial development planning of the planning experience of non-colonial, in certain cases economically and technically much more advanced countries, has of course still to be studied in detail, but to the author it seems at first sight to be high. The availability of such experience should make an especially useful contribution to a balanced view on that basic question with which no book can deal, but which every plan has to solve in broad outline as a premise to planning, namely the legitimate field of administrative planning in the economy to be planned.

Appendix I: Areas and Populations

TABLE I

BRITISH TERRITORIES[1]

Data in parentheses are in units

	Area in '000 square miles (to the nearest 1,000)	Population (latest mid-year estimate) in '000,000s (to the nearest 100,000)	Year
ALL TERRITORIES	1,960[a]	83·0[b]	
EAST AND CENTRAL AFRICA	1,088	25·9	
Somaliland Protectorate	68	·6	1952
Kenya	225	6·2	1956
Uganda	94	5·6	1956
Tanganyika	363	8·5	1956
Zanzibar and Pemba	1	·3	1955
Northern Rhodesia	288	2·2	1956
Nyasaland	49	2·6	1956
WEST AFRICA	497	40·4	
Gambia	4	·3	1955
Gold Coast (excluding Togoland)	79	4·3	1956
Togoland	13	·4	1956
Federation of Nigeria	373	33·4	
Northern Region	282	18·1	1956
Eastern Region	29	7·6	1956
Western Region	45	6·5	1956
Lagos (Federal Capital)	(27)	·3	1956
Southern Cameroons	17	·8	1956
Sierra Leone	28	2·0	1952

[1] Cf. *Cmd 195*, 1957.

APPENDIX I

TABLE I (*continued*)

	Area in '000 square miles (*to the nearest* 1,000)	Population (*latest mid-year estimate*) in '000,000s (*to the nearest* 100,000)	Year
EASTERN GROUP	130	11·0	
Federation of Malaya	51	6·3	1956
Singapore[c]	(224)	1·3	1956
Christmas Island	(62)	(2,050)	1955
Brunei	2	(65,300)	1955
North Borneo	29	·4	1954
Sarawak	47	·6	1955
Hong Kong	(391)	2·4	1956
MEDITERRANEAN	4	·9	
Cyprus	4	·5	1956
Gibraltar	(2¼)	(25,000)	1956
Malta and Gozo	(122)	·3	1955
WEST INDIES GROUP	100	3·5	
Barbados	(166)	·2	1955
British Guiana	83	·5	1956
British Honduras	9	(82,000)	1956
Jamaica[c]	4	1·5	1955
Cayman Islands	(100)	(8,160)	1955
Turks and Caicos Islands	(166)	(6,600)	1952
Leeward Islands	(423)	·1	
Antigua	(171)	(51,900)	1955
Montserrat	(32)	(14,300)	1955
St Christopher Nevis and Anguilla	(153)	(53,900)	1955
Virgin Islands	(67)	(7,680)	1955
Trinidad and Tobago	2	·7	1955
Windward Islands	(726)	·3	
Dominica	(305)	(62,100)	1955
Grenada	(133)	(88,200)	1955
St Lucia	(238)	(87,200)	1955
St Vincent	(150)	(75,900)	1955
WESTERN PACIFIC GROUP	25	·6	
Fiji	7	·3	1955
British Solomon Islands	12	·1	1953
Gilbert and Ellice Islands	(369)	(40,800)	1955
New Hebrides	6	(52,900)	1954
Pitcairn	(2)	(140)	1955
Tonga	(269)	(53,800)	1955

TABLE I (*continued*)

	Area in '000 square miles (to the nearest 1,000)	Population (latest mid-year estimate) in '000,000s (to the nearest 100,000)	Year
ATLANTIC AND INDIAN OCEAN	122	1·6	
Bahamas	4	·1	1955
Bermuda	(21)	(40,800)	1955
Falkland Islands[c]	5	(2,250)	1955
St Helena[c]	(47)	(4,760)	1956
Ascension	(34)	(170)	1952
Tristan da Cunha	(38)	(280)	1953
Aden Colony and Perim[d]	(80)	·1	1955[d]
Aden Protectorate	112	·7	1953
Mauritius and Dependencies	1	·6	1956
Seychelles	(156)	(40,400)	1956

[a] Excluding area of Falkland Islands Dependencies.
[b] Based on latest mid-year estimates for territories.
[c] Excluding Dependencies.
[d] Census of February 1955.

APPENDIX I

TABLE II

FRENCH TERRITORIES[1]

Data in parentheses are in units.

	Area in '000 square miles (to the nearest 1,000)	Population (latest mid-year estimate) in '000,000s (to the nearest 100,000)	Year
ALL TERRITORIES	3,236	32·6	
AOF: TOTAL	1,800	18·7	1955
Senegal	77	2·2	1955
Soudan	770	3·6	1955
Guinee	96	2·5	1955
C. d'Ivoire	126	2·5	1955
Dahomey	45	1·6	1955
Niger	464	2·3	1955
Mauritius	424	·6	1955
Haute Volta	107	3·3	1955
TRUST TERRITORIES: TOTAL	191	4·2	
Togo	22	1·1	1953
Cameroun	169	3·1	1954
AEF: TOTAL	981	4·7	1955
Gabon	104	·4	1955
Moyen Congo	134	·7	1955
Oubangui ch.	241	1·1	1955
Tchad	502	2·5	1955
OTHERS:			
Madagascar	230	4·6	1954
Comores	(780)	·2	1954
Côte des Somalis	(8,600)	(62,800)	1954
Nlle Caledonie	(7,400)	(63,100)	1954
Nlles Hebrides	(4,700)	(50,570)	1953
Est Frs. d'Oceanies	(1,600)	(52,670)	1951
St Pierre et Miquelon	(80)	(4,606)	1951

[1] Calculated from *Inventaire social et économique des territoires d'outre-mer, 1950–5*, 1957.

APPENDIX I

TABLE III

BELGIAN AND DUTCH TERRITORIES

	Area in '000 square miles (to the nearest 1,000)	Population (latest mid-year estimates) in '000,000s (to the nearest 100,000)	Year
Belgian Congo	916[1]	13·0[2]	1956
Ruanda-Urundi	21[1]	4·5[2]	1956
TOTAL	936	17·4	1956
Surinam or Dutch Guiana	56[3]	·2[3]	1953

[1] Cf. Jacques Lefebvre: *Structure économique du Congo Belge et du Ruanda-Urundi*, 1955, p. 9.
[2] Cf. *La situation économique du Congo Belge et du Ruanda-Urundi en 1956*, 1957, pp. 11, 19, 25.
[3] Cf. *Surinam in the Making*, 1955, p. 1.

Appendix II: Select Bibliography

I. BRITISH TERRITORIES

COMMAND PAPERS

Cmd 6174, West India Royal Commission, 1938-9; Recommendations, pp. 30 (1940).
Cmd 6175, Statement of Policy on Colonial Development and Welfare, pp. 8 (1940).
Cmd 6299, Certain Aspects of Colonial Policy in War-time, pp. 10 (1941).
Cmd 6422, Colonial Development and Welfare Act (1940), Report on the operation of the Act to 31st October 1942, pp. 14 (1943).
Cmd 6457, Reports for 1942-3, pp. 4 (1943).
Cmd 6532, Reports for 1943-4, pp. 16 (1944).
(Thereafter Reports are annual, under House of Commons papers.)
Cmd 6607, Report of the West India Royal Commission, pp. 480 (1945).
Cmd 6713, Despatch dated November 12, 1945, from the Secretary of State for the Colonies to Colonial Governments, pp. 12 (1945).
Cmd 7533, Colonial Office. Report of the British Guiana and British Honduras Settlement Commission, pp. 359 (1948).
Cmd 9375, Report on the Administration and Use of the Funds provided under the CD & W Acts, pp. 32 (1955).
Cmd 9462, Colonial Development and Welfare Act, 1955. Despatch dated April 26, 1955, from the Secretary of State for the Colonies to Colonial Governments, pp. 9 (1955).
Cmd 9475, East Africa Royal Commission 1953-5. Report, presented by the Secretary of State for the Colonies to Parliament by Command of Her Majesty, pp. 482 (1955).
Cmd 9801, Despatches from the Governors of Kenya, Uganda and Tanganyika and from the Administrator, East Africa High Commission, commenting on the East Africa Royal Commission 1953-5 Report, pp. 195 (1956).
Cmd 9804, Commentary on the despatches from the Governors of Kenya, Uganda and Tanganyika and the Administrator, East Africa High Commission, on the East Africa Royal Commission Report, pp. 6 (1956).
Cmd 195, The Colonial Territories 1956-7, pp. 185 (1957).
Cmd 237, The United Kingdom's Rôle in Commonwealth Development (1957).
Also: Colonial Territories Annual Reports, Colonial Office.

COLONIAL NUMBERED SERIES

Col. No. 184, Development and Welfare in the West Indies, 1940–2, Report by Sir Frank Stockdale, pp. 93 (1943).
Col. No. 187, Report of the West Indian Conference held in Barbados, March 21–30, 1944, pp. 21 (1944).
Col. No. 189, Report by Sir Frank Stockdale on Development and Welfare in the West Indies, 1943–4, pp. 115 (1945).
Col. No. 281/(1–7). An Economic Survey of the Colonial Territories, 7 volumes (1951–).

CENTRAL OFFICE OF INFORMATION REFERENCE PAMPHLETS

No. 13, Economic Development in the Commonwealth (1956).

CENTRAL AFRICA

Federation of Rhodesia and Nyasaland

Federation of Rhodesia and Nyasaland. Development Plans, 1954–7, in four volumes (1953).
Development Plan, 1955–9, presented to the Federal Assembly, June 30, 1955, pp. 7 plus tables (1955).

Northern Rhodesia

Northern Rhodesia. Ten Year Development Plan for; as approved by the Legislative Council on February 11, 1947, pp. 88 (1948).
Northern Rhodesia. Review of the Ten Year Development Plan of; submitted by the Development Authority and approved by the Legislative Council, June 1948, pp. 72 (1948).
Northern Rhodesia. Second (1951) Review of the Ten Year Development Plan of Northern Rhodesia, submitted by the Development Authority, and approved by the Legislative Council, November 1951, pp. 62 (1951).
Northern Rhodesia. Report of the Development Authority for the Year 1952, pp. 40 (1953).
Northern Rhodesia. Revision of the Northern Rhodesia Ten Year Development Plan, presented to the Legislative Council on November 30, 1953, by the Development Secretary, pp. 23 (1953).
Northern Rhodesia. Report of the Development Authority for the Year 1953, pp. 39 (1954).
Northern Rhodesia. Report of the Development Authority for the Year 1954, pp. 35 (1955).

Nyasaland Protectorate

Nyasaland Protectorate. Development Programme, 1931–4, pp. 65 (no date).
Nyasaland Protectorate. Report of the Post-War Development Committee, pp. 139 (1946).

Revised Report of the Post-War Development Committee, pp. 42 (1947).
Nyasaland Protectorate. The Nyasaland Development Programme, pp. 31 (1948).
Review of the Development Plan, 1946 to 1955, pp. 30 plus tables (1950).

EAST AFRICA

Kenya Colony

Interim Report on Development. Kenya, pp. 13 (1945).
Kenya. Report of the Development Committee. Volume i, pp. 140; volume ii, Appendices and Reports of Development Sub-Committees, pp. 80 (1946).
Kenya. Development and Reconstruction Authority Report, covering the period August 1, 1945, to December 31, 1945, pp. 41 (1947).
Annual Report of the Development and Reconstruction Authority, 1948, pp. 41 (1949).
Kenya. Ditto for 1949, pp. 40 (1950).
Kenya. Ditto for 1950, pp. 34 (1951).
Kenya. Report of the Planning Committee, pp. 114 (1951).
Kenya. Annual Report of the Development and Reconstruction Authority for 1951, pp. 31 (1951).
Kenya. Ditto for 1952, pp. 39 (1953).
Kenya. Sessional Paper No. 51 of 1955. The Development Programme, 1954–7, pp. vii, 126 (1955).
Sessional Paper No. 3 of 1945, Proposals for the Reorganization of the Administration of Kenya, pp. 10 (1945).
Cmd 9103, Kenya. Proposals for a Reconstruction of the Government, pp. 4 (1954).
Kenya. A Plan to Intensify the Development of African Agriculture in Kenya, pp. 75 (1954).

Tanganyika Territory

Tanganyika. An Outline of Post-War Development Proposals, pp. 59 (1944).
A Ten Year Development and Welfare Plan for Tanganyika Territory, Report by the Development Commission, pp. 67 (1946).
Annual Report of the Development Organization, 1949, pp. 18 (1950).
Ditto, 1950, pp. 18 (1951).
Revised Development and Welfare Plan for Tanganyika, 1950–6, pp. 40 (1951).
Annual Report of the Development Organization, 1951, pp. 57 (1952).
Ditto, for 1952, pp. 42 (1953).
Ditto, for 1953, pp. 44 (1954).
A Review of Development Plans in the Southern Province, 1953, pp. 47 (1954).
Tanganyika. Annual Report on Development, 1954, pp. 40 (1955).
Capital Works Programme. Development Plan, 1955–60, pp. 29 (1955).
Sir A. Gibb: Report on Central African Rail Link Development Survey. 2 vols. (1952).

Uganda Protectorate

Uganda Protectorate. Joint Report of the Standing Finance Committee and the Development and Welfare Committee on Post-War Development, pp. 130 (no date).
Uganda Protectorate. A Development Plan for Uganda, by E. B. Worthington, pp. 112 (1946).
Annual Development Report for period ending September 1947, pp. 22 (1947).
Progress in Uganda, 1948, pp. 34 (1949).
The 1948 Revision of the Plan by Sir Douglas Harris, pp. xvii, 146 (1949).
Progress in Uganda, 1949, Being portions of the Address by H.E. the Governor to the Legislative Council at the opening meeting of the Twenty-ninth Session on December 14, 1949, pp. 39 (1950).
A Five Year Capital Development Plan, 1955–60, pp. 73 (1954).
Report of Agricultural Productivity Committee, pp. 148 (1954).

WEST AFRICA

Nigeria

Sessional Paper No. 6 of 1945, Preliminary Statement on Development Planning in Nigeria, pp. 24 (1945).
Sessional Paper No. 24 of 1945, A Ten Year Plan of Development and Welfare for Nigeria, pp. 157 plus maps (1945).
Annual Report on the General Progress of Development and Welfare Schemes, 1948–9, Sessional Paper No. 20 of 1949, pp. 83 (1949).
Annual Report on the General Progress of Development and Welfare Schemes, 1949–50, Sessional Paper No. 22 of 1950, pp. 106 plus maps and charts (1950).
Annual Report on the General Progress of Development and Welfare Schemes, 1950–1, Sessional Paper No. 26 of 1951, pp. 124 plus maps and charts (1951).
A Revised Plan of Development and Welfare for Nigeria, 1951–6, pp. 146 (1951).
Report on the Work under the Development Plan carried out by the Public Works Department in the Northern Provinces, 1946–51, Kaduna, pp. 11 (1952).
Nigeria. Annual Report on the General Progress of Development and Welfare Schemes, 1951–2, pp. 132 (1953).
Nigeria. Annual Report on the General Progress of Development and Welfare Schemes, 1952–3, pp. 148 (no date).
The Economic Development of Nigeria (IBRD Report), John Hopkins Press, Baltimore, pp. 686 (1955).
The Economic Programme of the Government of the Federation of Nigeria, 1955–60, Sessional Paper No. 2 of 1956, pp. 75 (no date).
Development of the Western Region of Nigeria, 1955–60, Sessional Paper No. 4 of 1955, pp. 49 (1955).
Outline of Development Plan, 1955–60, Eastern Region of Nigeria, Sessional Paper No. 4 of 1955, pp. 8 (1955).
Northern Region of Nigeria, A Statement of Policy in the Development Finance Programme, 1955–60, pp. 31 (1955).

APPENDIX II

Gold Coast

A Ten Year Plan of Development and Welfare for the Gold Coast, pp. 57 (1946).
Progress Report for the period ended February 31, 1949, on the Draft Ten Year Plan of Development and Welfare, pp. 22 (Gold Coast, 1950).
Draft Ten Year Development Plan for the Gold Coast, pp. 409 (no date).
The Development Plan, 1951, approved by the Legislative Assembly, September 1951, pp. 34 (Gold Coast, 1951).
Development Progress Report for the Year April 1, 1952, to March 31, 1952, pp. 20 (1953).
Ditto, 1953, pp. 23 (1953).
Development Progress Report, 1955, pp. 46 (1956).
W. A. Lewis, Report on Industrialisation and the Gold Coast, pp. 23 (1953).

Gambia

Development and Welfare in the Gambia, Gambia No. 48 (June 1943).
The Gambia. Memorandum on Development, Sessional Paper No. 14/46, pp. 7 (1946).
The Gambia. Report on Development and Welfare, 1947, pp. 8 (1948).
Ditto, 1948, pp. 6 (1949).
Ditto, 1949, pp. 4 (1950).
The Gambia. Report on Development and Welfare, 1950–2, Sessional Paper No. 1/53, pp. 4 (1953).

Sierra Leone

An Outline of the Ten Year Plan for the Development of Sierra Leone, pp. 23 (1946).
Progress Report on the Development Programme for the year 1946, Sessional Paper of 1947, No. 3, pp. 7 (1947).
Progress Report on the Development Programme for 1947, Sessional Paper No. 7 of 1947, pp. 11 plus appendices (1947).
Progress Report on the Development Programme for 1948, Sessional Paper No. 16 of 1948, pp. 8 plus appendices (1948).
Progress Report on the Development Programme for 1949, Sessional Paper No. 6 of 1949, pp. 10 plus appendix (1949).
Ditto, for 1950, pp. 11, appendices (1950).
Ditto, for 1951, pp. 12, appendix (1951).
A Plan of Economic Development for Sierra Leone, by H. Childs, pp. 56 (1949).

INDIAN OCEAN

Aden Colony

Aden Colony and Protectorate, First Report of the Development Committee, pp. 39 (1947).
Aden Colony and Protectorate, Second Report of the Development Committee, pp. 20 (1949).

APPENDIX II 199

Aden Colony, Memorandum on Five Year Development Plan, 1952–3 to 1956–7, pp. 33 (no date).
Aden Developments—Summary (DB. 36040/2), pp. 6 (1952).

Zanzibar

Legislative Council of the Protectorate of Zanzibar, Sessional Paper No. 1 of 1946, Programme of Social and Economic Development in the Zanzibar Protectorate, for the Ten Year Period, 1946–55, pp. 35, plus appendix (1946).
Zanzibar Protectorate. Report on the Progress of the Development Programme for the years 1946–51, pp. 57 (1951).
Sessional Paper No. 8 of 1955. Programme of Social and Economic Development in the Zanzibar Protectorate for the Five Year Period 1955–9, pp. 16 (1955).

Somaliland

Somaliland Protectorate. Development Plan (Colonial Development and Welfare Acts, 1940 and 1945), pp. 18 plus appendix (1950).
A General Survey of the Somaliland Protectorate, 1944–50 (CD & W Scheme D.484) by John A. Hunt, pp. 203 (1951).
Somaliland Protectorate. Annual Review of the Development Plan, 1953, pp. 21 (1954).
Ditto for 1954, pp. 22 (1955).
Somaliland Protectorate. Financial Statement of Proposed Development, 1955–60, pp. 35 (no date).

Mauritius

Memorandum on Mauritius Development and Welfare Ten Year Plan Publication No. 33, pp. 10 (1946).
Mauritius. Development and Welfare Progress Report No. 4, pp. 10 (1948).
Fourth Report by the Committee appointed to review the Mauritius Development and Welfare Ten Year Plan, Publication No. 57, pp. 8 (1950).

Seychelles

Seychelles Ten Year Development Plan, Report of the Committee appointed to draw up a Ten Year Development Programme and to advise on various representations for the reduction of taxation, pp. 29 (1947).
Seychelles Five Year Development Plan, 1956–60, and Estimates of Revenue and Expenditure for the First Phase Year 1956, pp. 13 (no date).

SOUTH-EAST ASIA AND THE PACIFIC

Federation of Malaya

Draft Development Plan for the Federation of Malaya, No. 68 of 1949, pp. 20 (1949),

Draft Development Plan of the Federation of Malaya, pp. 174 (1950).
Progress Report of the Development Plan for the Federation of Malaya, 1950–2, pp. vi and 128 (1953).

North Borneo

North Borneo, Reconstruction and Development Plan for 1948–55, pp. ii, 128 plus appendices (1948).
Cmd 8080, The Colombo Plan, pp. 101 (1950).
Cmd 8529, The Colombo Plan, The First Annual Report, pp. 75 (1952).

Sarawak

Memorandum on Development in Sarawak, pp. 14 (1947).
Development Programme for Sarawak for the Period 1951–7 (1950).
Revised Development Plan of Sarawak, 1951–7, pp. 6 plus 2 appendix (1952).
The Natural Resources of Sarawak, pp. 38 (1952).
Sarawak, Report on Development, 1952, pp. 17 (1953).
Ditto, 1953, pp. 19 (1953).
Development Plan of Sarawak, 1955–60, pp. 53 plus map (1954).
Report on Development, Sarawak, 1955, paragraphs 85 plus appendices (1955).

Fiji

Fiji, Legislative Council Paper No. 24, of 1946, Report of Post War Planning and Development Committee, pp. 32 (1946).
Fiji, Legislative Council Paper No. 29, of 1949, Report of the Development Revision Committee, pp. 35 (1949).
Fiji, Legislative Council Paper No. 12, of 1953, Report of the Economic Review Committee, pp. 29 (1953).

THE WEST INDIES

Antigua Development Plans, pp. 66 (no date).
Barbados Development Plans: A Ten Year Development Plan for Barbados, and Sketch Plan of Development 1946–56, pp. 63 (1945).
Barbados. Five Year Plan of Development and Taxation, pp. 28 (no date).
Development Finance 1955–60, Barbados Requirements, pp. 15 (1955).
British Guiana. Memorandum on the Financial Position of British Guiana, 1920–46, with special reference to the Financing of Development and Welfare Schemes, 1947–56, by O. A. Spencer, pp. 122 (1946).
British Guiana. Papers relating to Development Planning, Legislative Council Paper, No. 8, General Ten Year Plan of Development and Welfare, 1947–56, pp. 70 (1947).
British Guiana, Fourth Legislative Council, No. 17, Second Session, address by H. E. Sir Charles Campbell Woolley, pp. 9, (1948).
British Guiana. 1955 Development Estimates, pp. 34 (1955).
Economic Development of British Guiana, IBRD Report, pp. xix, 366 (1953).

British Honduras. Report of the Development Planning Committee, 145 paragraphs (1946).
British Honduras. Draft Development Plan, pp. 65 (1950).
British Honduras. Development Plan. Immediate Plan, Part II, Sessional Paper 12/1952, pp. 58 plus appendices (no date).
The Economic Development Programme of British Honduras, IBRD, pp. 34 (1954).
Review of Progress in the Development and Welfare of the Colony of British Honduras during the period 1948–54, pp. 32 plus appendices (no date).
British Honduras. Development Plan, 1955–60, Revised Draft. Part III, pp. 48 (1955).
Grenada Development Plans. A plan for the development of the Colony of Grenada, 1946–56, Windward Islands, BWI, 171 paragraphs (no date).
Grenada. Revised Development Plan for Grenada 1950–6, pp. 18 (no date).
Jamaica. Report of Economic Policy Committee, Chairman Dr. F. C. Benham, pp. 45 (1945).
Jamaica. Memorandum on Colonial Development and Welfare Schemes, pp. 24 (1945).
A Ten Year Plan of Development for Jamaica, pp. 60 (1945).
Progress Report of Development (including Colonial Development and Welfare Schemes) for the year 1946, pp. 43 (1947).
A Ten Year Plan of Development for Jamaica, pp. 63 (1946).
Ditto, pp. 56 (1947).
Report on the Revision of the Ten Year Plan of Development for Jamaica, pp. 28 (1951).
Jamaica. Development Programme, 1954–5 to 1959–60, pp. 20 plus Appendices A–E (1954).
The Economic Development of Jamaica, IBRD Report, pp. xviii, 288 (1952).
Turks and Caicos Islands, Development Plan, printed by the Government Printer, Duke Street, Kingston, Jamaica, pp. 11 (1947).
Leeward Islands. Development Plan, pp. 160, appendices (1947).
Draft Ten Year Plan of Development, St. Christopher, Nevis and Anguilla in the Colony of the Leeward Islands, 1946–56, pp. 49 (1950).
Saint Lucia. Development Sketch Plan, 1946–50, pp. 27, appendices (1945).
Saint Lucia. Revised Development Sketch Plan, 1946–56, pp. 31 (no date).
Saint Lucia. Financial Survey, 1950, pp. 69 (1950).
Plan of Development for the Colony of St Vincent, Windward Islands, BWI, including the Preliminary Examination of the Economic and Fiscal Structure of St Vincent by Dr. A. L. Jolly, pp. xviii, 821 (1947).
Council Paper No. 2 of 1951, St Vincent Memorandum on the Revision of the Development Plan, pp. 26 (1950).
Memorandum showing progress of certain development schemes in the Colony of Trinidad and Tobago up to 1948. Laid before the Legislative Council on December 17, 1948, Trinidad and Tobago, pp. 19 (1949).
Trinidad and Tobago. Five Year Economic Programme, Parts I–V, Volume I. Laid in the Legislative Council on June 16, 1950. Trinidad and Tobago, pp. 55 (1950).

Trinidad and Tobago. Five Year Economic Programme, Appendices I–VII, Volume II. Laid in the Legislative Council on June 16, 1950, Trinidad and Tobago, pp. 112 (1950).

Trinidad and Tobago. Memorandum on Major Capital Works of Government as Planned in the Five Year Economic Programme. Showing Progress of Work in the Course of Execution and Work Proposed for 1955. As approved by the Legislative Council on December 8, 1954, pp. 55 (1954).

CYPRUS

Cyprus Development Plans, A Ten Year Programme of Development for Cyprus, pp. viii, 143 (1946).

Cyprus. Preliminary Planning Report by Sir Patrick Abercrombie, pp. 24 (1947).

Review of the Ten Year Development Programme for Cyprus, 1946–56, pp. 57 (1952).

II. FRENCH TERRITORIES

Le Premier Rapport de la Commission de Modernisation des Territoires d'Outre-Mer, pp. 136 (Janvier, 1948).

Reglementation Financière concernant la Réalisation des Plans d'Equipement et de Développement des Territoires d'Outre-Mer, pp. 84 (1950).

Deuxième Plan de Modernisation et d'Equipement. Rapport Général de la Commission d'études et de co-ordination des plans de modernisation et d'équipement des territoires d'Outre-Mer, pp. 187 (Avril, 1954).

Observations et Conclusions Personnelles du Gouverneur Roland Pré, Président de la Commission d'études et de co-ordination des plans de modernisation et d'équipement des territoires d'Outre-Mer, 2 vols (Mai, 1954).

Rapports annuels sur l'exécution du plan de modernisation et d'équipement de l'Union française (Metropole et Outre-Mer), (annually since 1955).

Ministère de la France d'Outre-Mer: Inventaire Social et Economique des Territoires d'Outre-Mer, 1950 à 1955 (1957).

CCFOM and FIDES, working papers, especially for 1955, 1956 and 1957.

Rapports Annuels du Gouvernement Français à l'Assemblée Générale des Nations Unies sur l'administration du Cameroun placé sous la tutelle de la France.

Gouvernement Général de l'AOF. Direction Générale des Services Economiques. Bulletin Economique Mensuel (since 1951).

Haut Commissariat de l'AOF. Bulletin Statistique Général (quarterly, since 1946).

Institut d'Emission de l'AOF et du Togo. Notes d'Information et Statistiques (periodical).

Ditto, Rapport d'Activité, Octobre 1955–Décembre 1956, pp. 154 (1957).

Haut Commissariat de l'AOF. Annuaire Statistique de l'AOF, (since 1950).

L. B. de Carbon. Les Plans Monétaires Internationaux. L'Investissement dans les Territoires Dépendants. Institut de Science Economique Appliquée, Cahiers Serie A., No. 8 and No. 9.
René Moreux. Principes Nouveaux d'Economie Coloniale, pp. 174 (1952).
Pierre Moussa. Les Chances Economiques de la Communauté Franco-Africaine, pp. 273 (1957).

III. BELGIAN TERRITORIES

Ministère des Colonies. Plan Décennal pour le Développement Economique et Social du Congo Belge, pp. 601 (1949).
Ministère des Colonies. Plan Décennal pour le Développement Economique et Social du Ruanda-Urundi, pp. 598 (1951).
Ministère des Colonies. Direction des Etudes Economiques. La Situation Economique du Congo Belge et du Ruanda-Urundi (annually since 1950, until 1957 published also in English).
Rapports Annuels sur l'Administration de la Colonie du Congo Belge, presentés aux Chambres Législatives.
Ministère des Colonies. Rapport sur l'Exécution du Plan Décennal du Congo Belge, pp. 66 (1953).
Le Plan Décennal après six ans d'existence, pp. 54 (1956).
Banque Centrale du Congo Belge et du Ruanda-Urundi. Rapport Annuel, 1952-3 (and annually since).
Jacques Lefebvre. Structures Economiques du Congo Belge et du Ruanda-Urundi, pp. 142 (1956).
Contribution à l'étude du problème de l'économie rurale indigène en Congo Belge. Special number of 'Bulletin Agricole du Congo Belge', volume xliii, pp. 267 (1952).
L'Agriculture en Congo Belge et en Ruanda-Urundi de 1948 à 1952, pp. 220 (1954).
Agriculture Congolaise, pp. 75 (1954).
Ministère des Colonies, Direction des Etudes Economiques. Les investissements au Congo Belge, pp. 92 (1955).
Le Conseil d'Administration et le Collège des Commissaires, Union Minière de Haut Katanga. Rapports Annuels (since 1950).
A. Marthoz. Le Problème de l'Energie Electrique au Katanga (1951).
Union Minière du Haut Katanga. Monograph, pp. 154 (1954).

IV. NETHERLANDS TERRITORIES

Surinam Planbureau: Surinam's Development Possibilities. Preliminary Report. Part I: Introduction. Part II: The Projects. Paramaribo—The Hague (1951).
Stichting Planbureau Suriname: Verzamelde Memoranda overgelegd aan de Missie naar Suriname van de Internationale Bank voor Herstel en Ontwikkeling in November 1951. Paramaribo—'s-Gravenhage (1952).
Stichting Planbureau Suriname: De grondslagen van een Tienjarenplan voor Suriname. Paramaribo—Den Haag (1952).
Surinam Recommendations for a Ten Year Development Programme, IBRD Report, pp. xxvi, 271 (1952).

APPENDIX II

Surinam Planning Bureau: Planning the future of Surinam. A short introduction to the Surinam Ten Year Development Plan. Paramaribo —The Hague (January 1953).

Surinam Planning Bureau: Ten Year Plan for Surinam. Surinam (October 1954).

Government of Surinam: Surinam in the Making. Paramaribo (1955).

Samenvattend Eindverslag van het Welvaartsfonds Suriname teven verslag over het jaar 1954. Uitgebracht ingevolge artikel 10 van de Wet Welvaartsfonds. Suriname (1955).

Stichting Planbureau Suriname: Tienjarenplan voor Suriname. Begroting met toelichting. Paramaribo, Suriname (for the years 1955, 1956 and 1957).

Stichting Planbureau Suriname. Verslag 1954–6 Tienjaren plan Suriname uitgebracht ingevolge resolutie van 15 Maart 1955—No. 669 (G.B. No. 40). Paramaribo (2 volumes) (1957).

INDEX

Abercrombie, Professor, 70
African Survey, Lord Hailey's, 81
Aggrey, Dr K., 161
Algeria, 185
Amery, L. S., 59
Antigua, 129
Antilles, Netherlands, 74, 75

Barbados, 67, 101, 102, 136, 152
Bathurst, Gambia, 152
Bauer, P. T., 145fn.
Belgian Congo and Ruanda Urundi (*see also* Wigny, Franck), 13, 17, 20, 21, 37, 45, 48, 64, 73, 74, 75, 86, 98, 102, 105, 109, 111, 131, 165, 170, 184
Benham, Prof. F., 18
Blum Government, 71
Borneo, North, 100, 127, 129, 132, 136
Bridgetown, Barbados, 152
British Guiana, 70, 101, 135
British Honduras, 18, 68, 70, 129, 135
For British Guiana *and* British Honduras Settlement Commission *see* Evans Commission

Caisse Centrale de la France d'Outre-Mer (CCFOM), 19, 85, 108, 131, 146
Cameroons, 17, 106, 173
Caribbean, 65, 145
Caribbean Federation, 66
Caribbean Commission, Anglo-American, 66, 185
Cayman Islands, 66
Central African Railway Link, 152, 165fn.
Chalmers Wright, F., 31
Childs, H., 70

Cocoa Marketing Board and Funds, Gold Coast, 115
Colombo Plan, 132fn., 185
Colonial Development and Welfare: funds, 111, 129, 130; grants, 18, 22; schemes, 110, 112, 116
Colonial Development and Welfare Fund, 63, 65, 66, 153
Colonial Development Act, 1929: 58, 59, 60, 71, 80
Colonial Development and Welfare Act, 1940: 60, 119, 125, 126, 150, 151
Colonial Development and Welfare Act, 1945: 61, 126, 130, 151
Colonial Development and Welfare Advisory Committee, 81ff.
Colonial Economic and Development Council, 83
Colonial Research Committee, 81ff.
Colonial Stock Act, 57
Comité Directeur (FIDES), 108, 156
Commissariat Général au Plan, 84, 108
Currency Boards, 22
Cyprus, 13, 18, 70, 96

Development and Reconstruction Authority (DARA), 90ff.
Duesenberry effect, 33
Dufferin and Ava, Marquis of, 82
Dutch East Indies—*see* Indonesia
Dutch Guiana—*see* Surinam

East Africa High Commission, 144
East Africa Royal Commission Report, 145fn.
Ecole Polytechnique, 64, 71
Ellison, E. W., 100
Empire Marketing Board, 58, 59

INDEX

Evans Commission (British Honduras and British Guiana Settlement Commission), 70, 129, 143

Farmers' Fund, 115, 130
Federation of Rhodesia and Nyasaland, 127
Firth, R., 31
Fleming, M., 54
Fonds d'Investissement et de Développement Economique et Social des Territoires d'Outre-Mer (FIDES), 19, 85, 108, 109, 110, 130, 131, 147, 154, 155, 156
Franck, J., 64fn., 73
French Equatorial Africa, 43, 106, 186
French Guinea, 48
French Imperial Economic Conference, 71, 72, 84
French Sudan, 43, 167; Niger Bend scheme, 72, 168, 171
French Union, 19, 73, 75, 108, 168, 169
French West Africa, 43

Gabon, 106
Gambia (*see also* Farmers' Fund), 97, 104, 107, 113, 115, 126, 130, 142, 152, 186
German Government, 72
Gezira, 171
Ghana, 64
Gibb, Sir Alexander, 165
Gibraltar, 13
Gold Coast, IDC, ADC, CMB, and their Funds, 97, 102, 108, 110, 113, 115, 119, 120, 121, 128, 150, 152, 161
Grenada, 18, 135
Grimble, Sir A., 66
Guggisberg, Sir G., 63, 150

Hague, The, 74, 75
Hailey, Lord, 81ff.

Hall, Rt. Hon. G. H., 82, 126, 140, 141
Harris, Sir Douglas, 133
Harris Plan, 116
Haute Volta—*see* French Sudan (Niger Bend scheme)
Henderson, Major A., 82, 83
Hong Kong, 14, 17
Hunt, John, 70

Imperial Economic Committee, 58
Imperial Economic Conference, 58
Indies, West—*see* West Indies
Indonesia, 74
Inga power development scheme, 109
International Bank for Reconstruction and Development (IBRD), 19, 20, 70, 74, 101, 131, 134, 155, 156, 185
Ivory Coast, 17, 173

Jamaica, 18, 67, 70, 100, 101, 126, 136, 172

Kenya, 18, 89ff., 95, 113, 114, 117, 119, 120, 121, 122, 127, 128, 129, 131, 133, 136, 144, 150, 154, 155, 157, 160, 161, 164, 169, 172, 173
Knight, Melvyn, 72
Kombo St Mary (Bathurst), 152
Kongwa scheme (Tanganyika), 171

Leeward and Windward Islands (*see also* St Vincent), 66, 133
Leopold, King, 73
Lewis Report, 48fn., 49fn.
London Money Market, 18, 19, 57, 142

MacDonald, Malcolm, 60, 63, 79, 81, 82, 83, 126, 139, 143
Macmillan, Harold, 82

INDEX

Malaya, 18, 95, 96, 101, 105, 119, 127, 138
Malta, 13, 18
Marshall, Alfred, 50, 51, 52
Mau Mau, 93, 131
Mauritius, 99, 114
Monde Coloniale, Le, 71fn.
Monnerville, Gaston, 84
Moore, Sir Henry, 89
Morocco, 72
Moussa, P., 13fn., 19fn.
Moyne, Lord, 60, 81: Commission, 60, 143, 144, 184; Report, 61

Netherlands Government, 20, 74, 86, 87, 109, 130, 156
Nigeria, 42, 64, 65, 70, 96, 101, 105, 107, 108, 110, 111, 112, 115, 119, 127, 128, 149, 155, 165
Nigerian Produce Marketing Boards, 115
North African Conference, 1923: 71
North African High Commission, 1935: 71
Northern Territories Railway (Gold Coast), 152, 166fn.
Nyasaland Protectorate, 64, 65, 119, 127

Orde Browne, Major, 158
Organisation and Methods (O & M), 185

Paish, Prof. F. W., 21fn.
Paramaribo (Surinam), 74
Pétain Government, 72
Pleven, R., 84
Pleven Plan, 73, 84, 85, 128
Point 4, President Truman's, 21
Portal, Viscount, 83
Pré, Roland, 85
Présence Africaine, 23
Prosperity Fund, 20, 74, 130

Railway projects in Africa, 165, 166, 167, 169
Rhodesia, Northern (*cf. also* Federation of Rhodesia and Nyasaland), 48, 95, 102, 105, 108, 113, 117, 119, 126, 134, 154, 158, 159, 161, 164, 168, 172, 173
Riley, B., 67fn.
Rothschild, J. A. E. de, 68
Rouch, J., 31fn.
Ruanda Urundi—*see* Belgian Congo

St Pierre et Miquelon, 14
St Vincent, 65, 133
Sarawak, 112, 120, 127, 130, 132
Sarraut, Albert, 71
Senegal, 42
Seychelles, 106
Shepherd, Prof. C. Y., 70
Sierra Leone, 70, 99, 107, 108, 113, 116, 121
Somaliland, 70
Soustelle, Jacques, 84
Spencer, O. A., 70
Stanley, Col., 62, 80, 82, 83
Stichting Planbureau Suriname, 74, 87
Stockdale, Sir Frank, 61, 62, 65, 66, 67, 68, 70, 82, 83
Sudan—*see* French Sudan, Gezira
Surinam, 13, 17, 20, 74, 75, 86, 87, 99, 101, 109, 130, 156, 171, 184
Swynnerton Report, 172

Tanganyika, 42, 99, 106, 113, 117, 118, 119, 127, 134, 142, 150, 158, 169, 171, 186
Tennessee Valley Authority (TVA), 54
Thomas, J. 58
Trans-Sahara Railway, 72
Trans-Zambezi Railway, 64, 167
Trinidad and Tobago, 65, 67, 108, 126, 154
Turks and Caicos Islands, 66

208　INDEX

Uganda (*see also* Harris, Harris Plan, Worthington), 42, 70, 95, 102, 104, 115, 116, 117, 119, 127, 128, 129, 131, 133, 155, 159, 164, 167, 168, 171, 172
Uganda African Development Fund, 116
Uganda Cotton and Coffee Price Assistance Fund, 116
Uganda Development Committee, 65
Uganda Development Council, 171
Uganda Productivity Committee, 171
Upper Katanga mines, 170

Volta River project, 152

West India Royal Commission (*see also* Moyne Commission and Report), 38, 60, 65, 118, 125, 138, 139, 143

West Indies, 15, 60, 61, 62, 65, 66, 67, 70, 100, 129, 135, 138, 139, 143, 149, 171, 172
West Indies Agricultural Policy Committee, 100
West Indies Economic Policy Committee, 100
West Indies Comptroller (*see also* Sir F. Stockdale), 100, 101
West Indies Financial and Economic Adviser, 133
Wigny, P., 98
Windward Islands—*see* Leeward Islands
Worthington, E. B., 70, 119, 159

Yamey, B., 145fn.
Young, Sir Hilton, 81fn.
Young, Prof. Allyn, 51, 52, 54

Zanzibar, 96, 141